THE INNER ROOM

I^{the}nner Room

A Journey into
LAY MONASTICISM

MARK PLAISS

ST. ANTHONY MESSENGER PRESS

Cincinnati, Ohio

Scripture citations are taken from the *New American Bible*, copyright
©1991, by the Confraternity of Christian Doctrine (CCD),
Washington, D.C.

Chapter Two, "The Argument," first appeared in *Cistercian Studies
Quarterly*, Summer 1999, under the title "Lay Monasticism."

Excerpts from Thomas Merton's *Journals of Thomas Merton*, copyright
©1997, used by permission of HarperCollins Publishers, Inc.

Excerpts from William of St. Thierry's *Exposition on the Song of Songs*,
reprinted by permission of Cistercian Publications.

Cover photographs by Connie Wellnitz;
    copyright ©2000, DigitalVision/PictureQuest
Cover design by Mary Alfieri
Book design by Sandy L. Digman

Library of Congress Cataloging-in-Publication Data

Plaiss, Mark.
    The inner room : a journey into lay monasticism / Mark Plaiss.
        p. cm.
    ISBN 0-86716-481-6 (pbk.)
    1. Monastic and religious life. 2. Laity—Religious life. 3.
Spiritual life—Catholic Church. I. Title.
    BX2435 .P58 2003
    255'.093—dc21
                                                    2002011485

ISBN 0-86716-481-6
Published by St. Anthony Messenger Press

www.AmericanCatholic.org

Printed in the U.S.A.

But when you pray, go to your inner room, close the door, and pray to your Father in secret. And your Father who sees in secret will repay you.

—MATTHEW 6:6

For SARA,
about whom Scripture says,

A worthy wife brings joy to her husband,
peaceful and full is his life.

A good wife is a generous gift
bestowed upon him who fears the LORD . . . .

— SIRACH 26:2–3

Table of Contents

1

Monastery Road

Dead of night.

Drunk on God, Merton and the Desert Fathers I punch the clutch and shift into fifth. Psalms, centering, silence, song, work, wonder, waiting, wisdom: I can't get there fast enough when "there" is available to me only once a year.

But is it? The books I read, the prayers I chant, the quiet I make already place me at that point of the universe where Terce, Sext and None are daily rounds of passage; where Vespers, Lauds and Compline make love with clouds of unknowing. Still, the spark is there, the tug is strong, the nudge is sharp: "Go. You must!" I obey an ancient call from God spoken before in the beginning. A call so deep and gorgeous and wild it overwhelms the siren calls of logic and ease.

So I crank up the heat, flip on the brights and follow the hypnotizing line of white past the cities and towns that dot the land between me and my hope and my God. It's just over the hill and around the curve and up the slope and . . .

I came flying off the Skyway and onto the Dan Ryan

Expressway at ten minutes after four in the morning, an hour after I had left the house back in La Porte, Indiana.

The night was clear. The stars that had sparkled so brightly in the black sky back home in Indiana, however, were replaced by the panorama of lights burning proudly in the skyscrapers of Chicago. The Chicago Transit Authority train spat sparks as it rumbled down the median of the expressway. When I neared O'Hare Airport, I noticed tiny points of light in the sky: too bright, too near and too numerous to be stars. They were airplanes stacked up in the sky approaching for landing at the world's busiest airport.

Art Bell was on WLS radio. This night his guest was a witch who proudly—and on a dare from a listener—cursed and denounced Jesus of Nazareth. I heard the witch's curse while tossing forty cents into the basket at the Des Plaines toll plaza.

Tossing in my last toll on the Northwest Tollway near Rockford, I hopped onto U.S. Highway 20 heading west. My Honda Civic, nearly a quarter-million miles strong, was humming along just fine. Now, when I glanced in the rearview mirror I began to see not just the headlights of cars but the pale light of dawn. And, as the sky around me turned from pink to orange to blue, I began to notice the fields of corn and hay filling with frost, and the layers of fog drifting in the valleys. Up and down, up and down, I felt as if I were on a roller coaster as I drove over the hills of Stephenson and Jo Daviess Counties. But what a view! Cattle grazed on the steep hills of green grass. Farms nestled in the bottoms. Houses perched on ridges. Hawks glided overhead in the crisp clear October air. I was excited, and I grew more excited the closer I drew to my destination.

Four and a half hours after leaving home, I crossed the Julien Dubuque Bridge spanning the Mississippi River and drove into Dubuque, Iowa. At the stoplight at the foot of the bridge I hung a left and headed south. In a half hour or so I would be there.

I followed U.S. 151 as it split off from U.S. 61 just south of Dubuque. Soon thereafter I turned right onto Monastery Road.

A couple of minutes later, a building swung into my view as I rolled down a hill that faded right. I could make out the roofline. Then, when I reached the bottom of the hill, the whole southern face of the stone quadrangle was visible behind the towering pine trees. I slowed the car and turned right into the long circular driveway.

I parked in front of the doors of the guest house. Finally, I had arrived. With a deep sigh I thanked God for the safe trip. I had driven over two hundred and sixty miles to get to New Melleray Abbey, a Trappist monastery founded by Irish monks in 1849.

I popped the trunk and pulled out my gear: a blue hard-shell suitcase, a canvas bag and a satchel full of books, papers and pencils. I slung the canvas bag over my left shoulder and, with the suitcase and satchel in hand, headed toward the door. I could hear the sounds of farm equipment rumbling in the distance.

The door to the guestmaster's office was closed. A little sign on the door announced that the brother would return at 8:30 A.M. The grandfather clock along the wall opposite the guestmaster's door said 8:05. I charged up the stairs to the third floor.

At the third-floor landing, I turned left and passed through a door bearing the sign: "Monastic Enclosure: Associates Only." Three of the four rooms were occupied. The fourth room, my room, was empty and the door was open. I entered.

Dropping my gear on the bed, I stepped to the window and yanked on the cord, raising the blinds. Sunlight splashed into the room. My window looked out onto the preau, or courtyard. Perfect.

Removing the gray hooded smock from the closet, I pulled it over my head and allowed it to fall to my upper thighs. I sat on the bed and removed my Reeboks. I withdrew from my canvas bag my slip-on sneakers. I was ready. I snatched up the key on the desk and left the room, closing the door behind me. Back down the steps I hurried. At the bottom of this stairwell was a locked door. I unlocked it with my key and stepped through.

Now in the cloister, I stood a moment taking in the inviting odor of cooked food. I went to the window looking out onto the preau. Now that I was on the ground level I could see beads of dew still clinging to the grass.

The door I had gone through gently clicked shut behind me. I walked a short distance and through another door.

I was in the abbey church. Light poured in through the pointed windows high above me. I glanced to my left—no one was in the guest area. I turned right and walked past the organ. The choir stalls were empty as well. Midway up the choir stalls I halted and made a deep bow toward the altar. Then, I stepped into the stalls to my left, opposite the organ. Finding my stall, I slipped in and knelt on the hard red tile floor. I would need the remainder of the day and much of the next to settle down. Not until late tomorrow would I begin to feel the rhythm of the house. For five days I would pray, work and live at this abbey. For the moment, however, I was merely thankful to be alone in the church of my monastic home.

2

The Argument

Among the myriad forms of Christian expression is the vocation of lay monasticism. The lay monastic is a layperson called by God to transform his or her life into one continuous prayer by using the tools normally associated with monasticism. The monastic tools are primarily Office (Liturgy of the Hours), lectio divina—or "holy reading"[1] —meditation, silence and solitude.

Lay monasticism is not readily recognizable among the laity. The lay monastic, in daily life, dons no habit, wears no distinguishing ornament, lives not in a monastery. The vocation is largely invisible, thereby rendering it incapable of promotion or recruitment. The parish pastor may issue an appeal for Eucharistic Ministers, but he is unlikely to issue a similar appeal for lay monastics. Further, the lay monastic is usually alone in the vocation, often even unaware of the presence of other lay monastics who may be near. Lay monasticism is essentially the embodiment of Jesus' admonition to "go to your inner room, close the door, and pray to your Father in secret" (Matthew 6:6).

Because the vocation is hidden, a person receiving the

call to it is often perplexed. It is possible to ponder whether to enter the priesthood or religious life, which are known quantities, but how can a person ponder something about which nothing is known? Consequently, the person stumbles through one door after another trying to follow the voice that calls. Books are read; spiritual directors are consulted. The person persists in the search, for he or she feels compelled to do so, a compulsion fueled by the urge to rest in God. As philosopher and theologian Raimundo Panikkar writes:

> One does not become a monk in order to do something or even to acquire anything, but in order to be. The monk does not become a monk just because of a desire. . . . It is not because one wills it that one becomes a monk. The monk is compelled. 2

This search often leads to a monastery. There the person discovers the rhythm of life that speaks to the soul: prayer, work, silence. This discovery is often accompanied by deep spiritual rumblings, a sense of being overshadowed. There may even be pangs of fear. What this person has experienced is God. What this person has uncovered is a vocation. The person has followed the voice, and the voice is monastic.

Now this person is thoroughly confused. Perhaps he or she is married, has children and is paying off a mortgage. How can all that be reconciled with this apparent call to monasticism? The monastery is for the canonical monk; monasticism is a lifestyle. In time, the person discovers that this conflict is an illusion, and realizes that he or she can be a monk as well, a lay monastic. It is as Paul Evdokimov, a writer on Eastern Christian spirituality and liturgy, writes:

> Monasticism creates a certain receptivity in the universal priesthood of the laity. The testimony of the Christian faith

in the framework of the modern world postulates the universal vocation of interiorized monasticism.... Today it [monasticism] makes an appeal to all, to the laity as well as to monastics, and it points out a universal vocation. For each one, it is a question of adaptation, of a personal equivalent.[3]

To realize the nature of this call to monasticism and to accept it are giant steps toward obtaining peace and solitude, for to accept one's identity is to be, to simply rest in God. Wherever the lay monastic may be, whatever the lay monastic may be doing, he or she is, thus, participating in the will of God. Thomas Merton writes:

> The monastic life demands first of all a profound understanding and acceptance of solitude.... But this capacity for solitude is nothing else than the full affirmation of one's identity, that is to say, the complete acceptance of oneself as willed by God and of one's lot as given by God.[4]

The canonical monk lives in community; the lay monastic often joins a community. Lay monastics in such a community are known as oblates or associates. These groups are attached to Benedictine or Cistercian monasteries, and these groups lend support, encouragement and prayer to the secular monk. Within the Cistercian and Benedictine families these associate and oblate groups are attached to particular houses. These groups meet periodically to share in singing, Office, lectio, silent prayer or some combination of these elements. The idea is to bolster the lay monastic, who usually practices her or his daily vocation in isolation from peers. These meetings allow contact with brother and sister lay monastics so that all can celebrate and rejoice in their vocation.

These associate and oblate groups are increasing in number and membership. Their growth is recognized and encouraged by both the Cistercians and Benedictines. In

1991, Father Armand Veilleux, then procurator general of the Order of Cistercians of the Strict Observance (O.C.S.O.), spoke at a conference in Kalamazoo, Michigan:

> Nowadays, a quite generalized phenomenon in the monastic world, as in the religious world in general, is that we find many lay people who feel called to a life of prayer and to a more complete dedication to God. They don't feel called to abandon their family, their job, their responsibilities in society. But are called to a deeper life of prayer and communion, and they feel a need to form small communities with other lay people. They also find a support and a nourishment for their spiritual life in a close relationship with a monastic community. . . . The first Cistercians were very creative in opening up monastic life again to lay people. I want to suggest that the challenge offered to the Cistercian Order nowadays, in a line of continuity with that original insight, would be to find ways to open up not only the wealth of Cistercian spirituality, but also the participation into the Cistercian communion to a post-Vatican II laity more and more aware of its dignity as laity and of its call to incarnate the contemplative ideal in the world today. [5]

One monastery, for example, that allows laity to participate in its community is New Melleray Abbey in Peosta, Iowa. Through its Monastic Center and its Associates of the Iowa Cistercians, New Melleray affords lay monastics a deeper involvement in the community. This is particularly so with the Monastic Center. The Monastic Center houses up to four men in a special wing of the guest house. Those in the Monastic Center may stay far longer than the normal retreat time of several days. Some stay just days, some weeks, others months. Fellowship with the community is offered by allowing the associates to follow the same schedule as the community. Work is required of the associates, and they are welcome in choir. Conferences are given to them at regular intervals. This balance of prayer, work,

Office and instruction, as taught and lived by the monastic community, provides the lay monastic with an example to live by upon leaving the monastery.

This is not to say that a monastery is the only place where such instruction or example can be obtained, only that the monastery is an obvious place for the lay monastic to explore his or her vocation. Furthermore, whether or not a monastery offers a program similar to New Melleray's Monastic Center, a monastery can still provide the lay monastic with a structure that he or she can emulate in the daily routine of life. Basil Pennington notes the importance of these structures:

> If it is true that the monk/nun needs structures that facilitate coming to fullness, and structures have a role in monastic life, a very important one, then the lay person, too, who wants to come to live the monastic dimensions of his or her life, needs facilitating structures that support this and open the way to it. And this we find lay people searching for today. It is something that is usually not found in the parish.[6]

Lay monasticism exists. The lay monastic may be married or single, man or woman, parent or not. The call to the vocation comes from God and is a means of union with God.

The monastery is a school where the lay monastic learns by both instruction and example the life of monasticism. That monastic life is, in turn, lived in the world, becoming a quiet, hidden, continuous prayer to God.

The monk is in the monastery. The monk is also on Wall Street, on Main Street and down on the farm. In years to come, the differentiation between *lay* and *monk* may perhaps disappear. As Bernardo Olivera, abbot general of the O.C.S.O., writes:

> Perhaps in a few years it will be out of style to speak of charismatic associations. The Spirit breathes where it wills,

but its work is always a work of communion. Will we see the day when we speak of "charismatic communions" in reference to the communion between cenobites and lay people in the same charism?[7]

The Holy Spirit is expanding the horizon of what it means to be a monk in order to bring all closer to the ultimate reality—Jesus the Christ.

NOTES

[1] For a full discussion of *lectio divina*, see pages 80-83.

[2] Raimundo Panikkar, *Blessed Simplicity: The Monk as Archetype* (New York: Seabury, 1982), p. 11.

[3] Paul Evdokimov, *Les ages de la vie spirituelle* (Paris: Desclee de Brouwer, 1964; new ed., 1995), as quoted by Michael Plekon, "'Interiorized Monasticism': A Reconsideration of Paul Evdokimov on the Spiritual Life," American Benedictine Review 48 (1997), p. 241.

[4] Thomas Merton, *Contemplation in a World of Action* (Garden City, N.Y.: Image, 1973), pp. 93-94. Emphasis added.

[5] Armand Veilleux, "Apologia De Barbis," O.C.S.O. Internet Homepage, www.ocso.org/net/layas-en.htm

[6] Basil Pennington, "Monastic Structures and Adaptation," in Raimundo Panikkar, *Blessed Simplicity: The Monk as Archetype*, p. 165.

[7] Bernardo Olivera, "Reflections on the Challenge of 'Charismatic Associations,'" *Cistercian Studies Quarterly* 32 (1997), p. 231.

3

First Visit to a Monastery

In the summer of 1977, I was a graduate student at Indiana University in Bloomington. The popular image of Indiana is one of a flat land filled with corn and hogs encircled by a ribbon of racetrack called the Indy 500. Those who hold such an image of Indiana have never visited Southern Indiana.

From Bloomington south to the Ohio River the land rises and falls in deep valleys and gorges. Forest pervades the countryside. The earth is clay, not the black dirt of fertile Central and Northern Indiana. Limestone and coal are plentiful. Southern Indiana is not as populous as the northern two-thirds of the state, and Evansville is the only city of size in the region. While the people of Central and Northern Indiana trace their ancestors back to settlers from Ohio, Pennsylvania and New England, folks in Southern Indiana come from Kentucky and the Carolinas. As for the Indy 500, well, that's for folks up north. And because Southern Indiana lies in the Ohio River valley, the summers there tend to suffer from the three Hs: haze, humidity and heat.

In that summer of 1977, I was newly married. My bride and I were living in married housing on campus. Married housing meant many things, but most of all it meant no air conditioning. Now, July in Bloomington can be downright miserable, newly married or not. So one blazing hot afternoon, in a desperate ploy to beat the heat, I walked the mile from married housing to the library—which was air-conditioned.

Having no pressing class work, I decided to browse the stacks and found myself on the floor where books on religion were housed. I was not looking for anything in particular, nor was I hunting for any given subject, I was merely browsing. Making my way through the stacks, I came across a blue, cloth-covered book, which I pulled from the shelf and flipped through, landing on the title page, where I came across a photograph. It was a black and white photograph of a large barn in a bucolic setting. Incongruously, several men in dark robes were sitting on benches in front of this barn. These men, I realized, were monks. They were sitting with their hands folded in their laps and their heads bowed, the hoods of the robes up over their heads. It appeared to me that their heads were bowed not so much in prayer as in obedience or fear. Standing at the door of the barn were two more monks in white robes, obviously photographed in the middle of a conversation. They were facing one another and gesturing with their hands. My first reaction upon seeing this photograph was to wonder what these monks were doing in front of a barn.

I began leafing through the pages and discovered a daily schedule the monks followed. They rose at 2:00 in the morning and went to sleep at 7:30 at night. Between those times they worked and came together for "Offices" bearing strange sounding names: Matins, Lauds, Prime, Terce, Sext, None, Vespers, Compline. In the book I saw more black and white photographs: a monk operating a bulldozer; monks in choir stalls, each in a deep bow; a monk celebrating Mass.

I was intrigued. I carried the book downstairs and checked it out and carried it home. Walking back to the apartment I could not help scanning through the pages. For the next couple of weeks I carried this book with me to my classes. When class grew dull—and what graduate program is not riddled with ennui—I would delve into monk-dom. I showed the book to several of my classmates, none of whom seemed even remotely interested. I also recall walking to and from the library in the humidity, my nose in this book scrutinizing the photographs and wondering how the monks could survive walking around in such heat in those robes. I found all this a welcomed reprieve.

The book was *The Waters of Siloe*, and the author was Thomas Merton.

The irony was that I was born and raised within an hour's drive of Merton, but I had never heard of him or the monastery in which he had lived—Gethsemani—until I was in graduate school.

My hometown, New Albany, sits on the north bank of the Ohio River across from Louisville, Kentucky. After moving to Bloomington, my wife and I made frequent weekend trips back to New Albany. On one of these trips back home, I decided I needed to find this monastery.

My wife was unwilling to travel with me to see a bunch of monks, so I enlisted my younger teenage brothers to accompany me. At the last moment, my grandmother decided she would like to come along as well. Having been born near Bardstown, Kentucky, she was lured, not by curiosity about the monastery, but by the knowledge that I would be traveling through Bardstown on my way.

An hour later, I was coasting to a stop along the avenue

of tall sweet gum trees lining the driveway at Gethsemani. As I stepped out of the car, I was immediately struck by the silence. Slamming the car doors shut seemed an intrusion. But who was I intruding upon? Nobody was in sight.

We followed the signs pointing the way to the church. After we climbed some stairs, our journey ended when we opened a door leading to the balcony overlooking the great church. At the railing, we saw, far below us, choir stalls, and at the far end of the church the altar. In the rounded end of the church, which I later learned was called the apse, burned the single vigil candle. My first impression on seeing this interior was that it bore no resemblance to the photographs of it in *The Waters of Siloe*, which had shown altars, statues and a gothic ceiling. The church I was in appeared to be totally different. The whitewashed walls were completely bare. The long part of the church, the nave, carried the choir stalls, and a modest ambo, or pulpit, stood between the stalls. A simple image of the Virgin stood to the side of the stalls. At the far end of the church was the stone altar and around it were some plain metal chairs. That was it for decoration.

My second impression had to do with the church's size—it was big. The nave seemed to go on and on. The vigil candle at the far end was a mere speck. The ceiling towered high over my head, and I was in the balcony. The exposed beams only accentuated the sense of vast space, of openness. Also, there was the silence. I had never been in a building, never mind a church, that was so quiet. The slightest noise seemed to reverberate throughout the place.

The church was empty save for a lone monk. Far below us he knelt, not in the choir stalls, but on the stone floor. His back was turned to us, and he was facing the altar. For several minutes we stood in the balcony and watched that lone monk not move a muscle.

Now my grandmother, a staunch Baptist, began peppering me with questions. She was trying to whisper these questions to me, but her whispers—always loud—seemed to ricochet off those whitewashed brick walls. "Is that a monk? Why is he here all alone? Aren't there others? Why is he kneeling there like that?" Since Vespers, or evening prayer, was well over an hour away, I decided it would be best to drive the short distance back to Bardstown to have a meal, and then come back for Vespers. During that time I could answer my grandmother's questions, and that poor monk could pray in peace.

So that is what we did.

About an hour later we returned to the abbey. We climbed back up the stairs to the balcony. We saw no one else was in the balcony, but when we peered out over the vast expanse of the church, the monk was still there praying. He had not moved, not an inch. He was in the exact same position and posture as when we had left for Bardstown. And he was all alone down there. My grandmother was flabbergasted upon seeing this, and in a loud voice that rolled like thunder down the long nave of the church she cried, "Why, Mark, he's still *there!*" To that monk's credit, he did not move an inch. Did not even flinch. But that was it for me. I spun around on my heels and headed for the door, my brothers right behind me. Bringing up the rear was my grandmother, all agog about the motionless monk.

Such was my first visit ever to a monastery.

4

The Monastic Center

About two years passed before I returned to Gethsemani. Time on our trips to New Albany was tightly scheduled, with visits to both sets of our parents who lived there, side trips to Gethsemani did not fit into the plan. By 1988, however, my spiritual reading had grown more and more monastic. Merton continued to provide a never-ending wealth of information and inspiration. Basil Pennington caught my attention, and then I discovered a publisher called Cistercian Publications, which turned out to be a gold mine of monastic writings.

I decided I needed to make a retreat. Gethsemani seemed the only logical place for me to do so, and so, on the weekend after Thanksgiving in 1988, I drove there for that purpose. It did not go well. I was anxious. I was confused by the Offices. I would stay up until my usual bedtime, 11:00 or 11:30 p.m., then attend Vigils at 3:15 in the morning. For the remainder of the day I would be dragging with sleepiness. I grew bored. Finally, I just went home.

I was discouraged, but not disheartened nor disillusioned. I continued to go back for annual retreats. Each time I went there, I felt more relaxed, more at home. Each time, I learned something new, and the Offices no longer confused me. I took long walks on the monastic property west of Highway 247 that runs past Gethsemani. I walked deep into those woods and allowed the silence to seep into my bones, into my being. I would go so deep into the woods that I could no longer hear traffic along the highway or the bells tolling at the monastery. Never did I come across other retreatants while on these walks. I was alone with God in the deep woods of Central Kentucky, and it was there in those woods that I discovered that the sound of God's voice can be silence.

I was no longer bored. In fact, the weekends now did not seem long enough. Just as I was getting settled in, feeling the rhythm of the house, it was time to leave. But there was so much more to learn! So much more of God to experience! So much more time to become lost in the woods!

The pivotal year was 1995. In September of that year, I was on retreat at Gethsemani from Wednesday, September 13, through Friday, September 15. I arrived at nine o'clock on that Wednesday morning. I can recall straining my neck to see the monastery as I drove down the last stretch of Highway 247 before it suddenly sweeps into view on the left. After checking in, I stepped into the church to give thanks for my safe arrival and to plead for a good retreat. Then I climbed St. Joseph Hill, across from the parking lot. Atop this hill is a statue of Saint Joseph holding the child Jesus. I sat in one of the chairs there and looked out over the countryside. All was quiet. The day was overcast, but humid, and mist waffled through and around the small, rounded hills known as the Central Kentucky knobs. Occasionally, a car passed on the highway below. I could see it coming a long way off. Then I would hear its tires singing on the pavement. Finally, it would zoom past me, and I would watch it disappear in the distance as it made its way toward the tiny villages of New Hope or New Haven.

Feeling drawn to the church, I walked back down the hill and headed that way. It was eleven o'clock when I entered, for the bells in the tower chimed the hour. The big old church was empty. I sat against the whitewashed brick wall in a chair by the railing that separates the guest area from the monastic area.

I sat there for some time, not praying with words, but praying by simply entering into the silence of the place. I do not know how long I had been sitting there when I *suddenly* became aware of God's presence. I heard no voice, saw no vision, felt no physical touch, but the presence of God was undeniably there, not just *there*, but *with* me and *in* me. My eyes grew wider, my heart raced, I broke into a sweat and my breathing became so rapid I was almost panting. I felt fear. Not fear as in dread or being in eminent danger, but fear as in realizing that I, a sinful man, was in the presence of the Holy, that God was truly present. But that fear left me as quickly as it had come. I remained sitting there stunned. I can only describe the experience as being overshadowed by God. I received no message, did not instantly discover the meaning of life, nor did I suddenly have all the answers to life's questions. But the experience was real. There is absolutely no doubt in my mind that God had left his mark upon me. Never before or since have I experienced God so intimately, so powerfully, so deeply. I sat in that chair bewildered and pleased, time seemingly suspended and unimportant. Soon the choir stalls before me and the chairs in the guest area around me began filling up. It was time for Sext, one of the daytime prayers, along with Terce and None. I cannot recall anticipating an Office so fervently in my life.

Following that experience, the two-day retreat became

totally inadequate. Gethsemani offers a five-day retreat as well, Monday through Friday. I decided that the following year I must take advantage of that.

So I did. My 1996 five-day retreat at Gethsemani was scheduled for Monday, September 30, through Friday, October 4.

Sara, our boys and I drove to Indianapolis on the Sunday before in order to witness the baptism of our nephew, Luke. That afternoon I drove on to New Albany and spent the night at my parents' house there.

The following morning, I rose at 5:30 and prayed the Office in my room. When I left the house at 6:30, it was still dark and my parents were still asleep.

I stopped in Louisville for a seven o'clock Mass and breakfast, then sped onto I-65 South. I was very excited now. I exited I-65 at Highway 245, noticing the odor of bourbon from the Jim Beam distillery just down the road, and drove through Bardstown. When I descended the final hill on my approach to Gethsemani, mist was rolling through the trees and fields around me. I broke past the trees on Highway 247, and there was the monastery—shrouded in fog the sun was trying to burn away.

Pulling into the driveway, I coasted slowly down the avenue of sweet gum trees. The parking lot was full. I saw cars with plates from Illinois, Ohio, Tennessee, Indiana, Michigan, Pennsylvania and, of course, Kentucky.

At the desk in the guest house was a monk in a motorized scooter, who asked loudly, "Have you come to join us?" He said, "We need men here." I told him I was scheduled for retreat. I signed in, and he gave me room 200.

The next five days flew by. Never was I bored. Never did I want for something to do. I prayed, meditated, wrote, read and tramped through the woods.

In the late afternoon of my final full day there,

Thursday, October 3, I prayed the Stations of the Cross that are located on the west side of the house. When I reached the fourteenth station I made my petition, if it were God's will, then I sat in a chair beneath some trees. I looked at the great fortress of God rising confidently from the hill on which it stands, its bells tolling, telling the surrounding hills and valleys and trees and grass that Jesus Christ is Lord. I sat there and prayed the rosary while a hawk floated high above those pealing bells.

Although that retreat at Gethsemani was wonderful to me, there was something missing. I was convinced that monastic spirituality was the avenue God was leading me down; however, I questioned if Gethsemani was the house for that monastic outlet. Something at Gethsemani left me feeling incomplete. I decided that I needed an experience at another house.

I got my chance in July of 1997. My older son had earlier that year received the sacrament of confirmation. As part of his confirmation gift, I arranged for us an overnight retreat together at New Melleray Abbey.

Why New Melleray? First, I had inquired at Gethsemani about bringing my fourteen-year-old son there along with me, and was told that their policy did not permit children of my son's age to make a retreat there. Second, it was the nearest Cistercian house besides Gethsemani. Plow through Chicago, then skim across the northern tier of Illinois into Dubuque, Iowa, and you are there. Leave early enough in the morning, and the drive through normally congested Chicago would be a snap. Third, New Melleray had something I was very interested in seeing: the Monastic Center.

I discovered the Monastic Center on the Internet. I had heard of New Melleray, and had pulled up its home-page for more detailed information about the house. When

I read there the description of the Monastic Center I nearly fell off my chair in excitement. The Monastic Center was exactly what I was looking for: a house relatively close by that would allow me to go beyond the normal offering of a retreat. According to the information on the homepage, the Monastic Center would give me instruction, assign me work side by side with the monks, allow me in choir and allow visits longer than the standard weekend or five days. My excitement upon discovering this place was real and sustained; I felt that perhaps this was where God wanted me to be.

So, in the wee hours of the morning of July 30, my son and I headed for New Melleray. We traveled through the night across northern Illinois and arrived at New Melleray about 8:30 A.M.

We were given room 316 in the guest house. My initial reaction to the place was that it compared unfavorably to the guest house at Gethsemani. Here at New Melleray, the halls were dark and the walls of the rooms were merely painted cinder blocks. There was an odor, though not foul, that was moldy and unpleasant. Obviously, the guest house at New Melleray was much older than the one at Gethsemani, which had been newly constructed in 1988. Comparisons between the two were unfair.

If my initial reaction to the guest house was displeasure, my reaction upon entering the church for the first time was delight. Like Gethsemani, and in the ancient tradition of Cistercian abbeys, New Melleray's church was without adornment. But the plain stone walls signified strength, vitality and warmth, and natural light from the many windows bathed the church.

Terce, at 9:15, was the first Office for my son and me. The church organ was close to the guest area, just on the other side of the iron railing that divided the guest area from the remainder of the church. Because of the close proximity of the organ, singing the hymn and psalms was made easy, and I sang along with gusto. After Terce was prayed, my son and I left, only to be met outside the door to the church by the monk who had been the organist. Brother Organist politely asked me if I would tone down my singing. "I'm closer to you than I am to them," he said, indicating the monks in choir, "and I need to hear them to follow along." The poor man fell all over himself trying to assure me he did not mean me to *stop* singing, but just to be less enthusiastic about it. This was the first time I had ever been reprimanded by a monk!

Later that day, I inquired of the monk at the desk of the the guestmaster's office about the Monastic Center. He took my name and room number, telling me that Brother Gilbert, who ran the Center and was in town that day, would contact me later.

Later in the afternoon, as my son and I chatted in our room, a knock came at the door. It was Brother Gilbert, who led me to a conference room down the hall where we could speak in private. I told him of my interest in the Monastic Center. I told him about my retreats at Gethsemani, that I was looking for something deeper and that the Monastic Center appeared to be what I was looking for. He asked me some general questions—where I was from, what parish I attended and so on—and said that the Monastic Center attracted a wide variety of men, both lay and clergy, from nearby and far away. When I explained to him where La Porte, Indiana, was located, he said there was a priest from Kalamazoo, Michigan, about one hundred miles east of La Porte, who came to the Monastic Center.

Our meeting was short, for Vespers was coming up at 5:30, and he was still not in habit, having come directly to my room from his appointment in town. He assured me that he saw no reason why I could not come to the Monastic Center and gave me an application to fill out. I told him that I would have it for him the next day. We stood, shook hands and he was off. Later, when my son and I left our room to go to Vespers, we walked down the third-floor hall to reach the stairwell. At the end of the hall, there at the top of the stairs, was a door with a sign that said, "Monastic Enclosure: Associates Only." Soon, I thought to myself, I would be an associate and be able to walk through that door.

The retreat with my son was memorable. We talked and prayed together and took walks around the property. We prayed psalms together. On our drive back home to La Porte we stopped at the observation tower just west of Elizabeth, Illinois. We climbed to the top of the tower and looked out over the rolling hills of Jo Daviess County, and commemorated the day and our experience by taking several pictures of each other. Prior to leaving New Melleray, I had given the application to Brother Gilbert and told him I would be in contact with him soon about my returning to the Monastic Center.

I returned on September 22. My first experience at the Monastic Center, however, was not good. As my first retreat at Gethsemani had been sub par, so my first retreat at the Monastic Center left much to be desired. First, the three other men in the Center with me were single and aspirants to the community. I, a married man with children, felt out of place and somewhat foolish among them. Further, returning so soon after my first visit made me feel guilty about being away from home. Finally, I questioned myself, wondering, when it came time for work, why a man would burn vacation time from his place of employment in order to go to another place and pull weeds from a garden.

Yet, just as with Gethsemani, I was not disheartened or

disillusioned with the Monastic Center. Something pulled me back and back again. I came back many times, and with each visit I felt more at home, more relaxed and convinced that this was the place for me. Much of my ease with the place can be attributed to three men I met there: Paul, Bill and Matt. Not only were these men roughly my age, but each possessed a good sense of humor. They were obviously interested in monastic life and took it seriously, yet they did not ooze phony seriousness. They were content to be themselves; they did not strive to mold themselves into stereotypical versions of the monk: head bowed, ponderously solemn, never speaking a word. I enjoyed working and laughing with them and discussing things with them. At the time I first met them, both Paul and Bill were considering seeking entrance to the community as postulants. Paul was from St. Louis. Bill had spent years teaching in Korea. Matt was married and lived in Wisconsin. Though it would be untrue to say that we are all friends, we are acquaintances, and I have learned much from them by simply observing them.

So what is this Monastic Center? The purpose of the Center is to offer men (and for now, only men) an opportunity to go more deeply into prayer by allowing them to participate more intimately in the life of the community. Men in the Monastic Center, called associates, work and pray right along with the community. The associates are given conferences on prayer, the psalms, *lectio divina*, the Office and the Rule of Saint Benedict. Associates are expected to follow the rules of the house on silence. This means no talking after Compline until after Mass the next morning. At all other times conversation is kept to a minimum. The idea is that this exposure to intense monastic spiritual life, as it is truly lived, will be adapted to the associate's everyday circumstances when he returns home.

The associates are housed in a special section on the third floor of the guest house called the Monastic Center. Each of the Center's four guestrooms has windows looking out on the front parking lot or on the preau and contains a simple bed, a desk with a chair, a second chair and a closet. There are a communal shower, toilet and lavatory and a small library and a small kitchen. One finds, lying on the desk of a guestroom in the Monastic Center, a key. This key is not a room key but a key to the cloister. This key gives the associate access to choir in the church. The Monastic Center clearly occupies a space between the general retreat house and the dwelling of the monks living there. No fee is charged, nor is there a time limit on how long one may stay. Men who aspire to join the community, such as Paul and Bill, often spend months there.

5

Vigils

At three o'clock in the morning my alarm clock beeps me awake in the Monastic Center. I roll out of bed and waddle into the bathroom, where I splash water on my face in order to wipe seven hours of sleep out of my eyes. My mind somewhat clearer now, I quickly dress. Before leaving my room, I slip the gray hooded smock over my head, making sure the hood lies flat against the back of my neck.

I leave my room and descend several flights of stairs, stopping at one landing to see a full October moon spill its light through a window. I continue down the stairs until I reach a large wooden door. With my key I open the door and step through. I am now in the cloister of the monastery.

All is quiet in these small hours of the night, very quiet and I am self-conscious about the noise when the door clicks shut behind me. The cloister is cool, the heat in the monastery has yet to be fired up, and I pat myself on the back for having had the foresight to wear a sweater under my smock. The cloister is also dimly lit, and at the far end of the cloister I can barely discern a silent figure approaching me. The figure is clothed in a white cowl with the hood up, making it impossible for me to see his face. The long sleeves of the cowl nearly drag the floor. Suddenly the shadowy figure turns to my left and disappears through a doorway.

I follow the figure through the doorway and find myself in the church. It is even darker there, the only light a dim one at the far end of the nave in the guest area, which, at this time of night, is empty of guests. I turn toward the altar and make a deep bow.

Next, I carefully make my way down the row of choir stalls that line the north wall of the church. There is a problem, however. I literally cannot *see* where I am supposed to sit, my assigned choir seat, because of the darkness. Moonlight is pouring through the windows high above me, but that is not enough light for me to find my way. I seek some sort of landmark—window, certain books on the stand, anything—that will give me a clue to where exactly I am to sit, but I can only hazard a guess. I select an empty stall I believe might be mine. I kneel on the tile floor and face the altar. After a minute or so of thanksgiving, I gather myself up and sit in my stall. I smile at the moonlight flooding through the windows high above the choir stalls along the south wall of the church and splashing onto the floor between the two choirs.

More monks enter the church and take their seats in choir. Presently, a monk comes walking down the length of the north choir. I notice he does not hesitate about finding his place. He confidently takes the stall next to mine. I instantly realize I am in the wrong spot, for my neighbors in choir are not monks but Monastic Center seculars. I slip down one choir stall, and I am relieved that I am most likely in the right place.

Someone coughs; another blows his nose. All this echoes off the stone walls and tile floor. I close my eyes and take some deep breaths in order to calm myself. Then ever so gently I begin saying to myself the Jesus Prayer: "Lord Jesus Christ, Son of God, have mercy on me, a sinner." Eventually I allow the prayer to drift out of my mind, and I experience the peace and center of faith.

The lights snap on. Now a sea of white robes rise. I, too, stand. We begin organizing the three books that are before us on the stand. I flip through the pages of the antiphonary until I find the appropriate page: Sunday, odd-numbered weeks. On this page I find not only the antiphons that will be chanted but also the psalms to which those antiphons are coupled. Next, I turn to the large psalter and find the appropriate psalm, in this case Psalm 17. Finally, I glance at the ordo sheet, which outlines the liturgical action and the sequence of its component parts, to determine which hymn will be sung. After I have my books in order, I turn and face the altar. The monks do the same. It will come any moment now.

At 3:30 the bell in the tower bongs in the dark silence of the dead of night. Upon its last peal, a lone voice, the cantor, chants, "O Lord, open my lips." The monks and I respond with, "And my mouth will proclaim your praise." Twice more the cantor invokes the Lord to open his lips, and each time the monks and I make the same reply.

Vigils has begun.

Vigils has the potential to be the most powerful of the Hours and, at the same time, the most boring and aggravating. To the newcomer in the life, Vigils is the perfect expression of monasticism: praying to God in the dead of night, a beautiful time of silence and peace, hearing and feeling the Almighty in the depths of darkness. But for one who has been there a while, Vigils can be drudgery. André Louf, Trappist monk and former abbot, puts it this way:

The calm of the night does not long remain a peaceful invitation to prayer. It becomes oppressive, inviting the novice in a thousand ways to escape. All the activities of the day start to occupy his mind before their time with a demanding urgency. And there seems much to be said in favor of a return to his own room for a further short sleep. Surely, he will be better able to meet the coming day after some extra rest? These suggestions do not come to him as idle insinuating thoughts, but with strength which will overpower him if he hesitates at all. In this way he discovers the ambivalence of his own heart. He cannot see any sign of determination and will which were so evident earlier. He discovers how little the night vigils attract him, though formerly he saw them as one of the most beautiful elements of the monk's life. Now they are only a nuisance. [1]

I often wonder how my view of Vigils would change if I were here every day for the rest of my life, and how I would confront that change.

Vigils is divided into two nocturnes. Nocturne I consists of three psalms, a reading and meditation. Nocturne II is three more psalms, another reading and more meditation. The meditation is done in the dark. Vigils is the longest of the Hours, usually lasting from forty to fifty minutes. It can run longer on the special days of the church known as solemnities.

What follows Vigils is equally as important as the Office itself; this is the time for meditation and prayer. With Vigils ending around 4:15 in the morning, there are over two hours before Lauds commences at 6:30 A.M. Here, in the quiet of the night, meditation and *lectio* actually continue the Office that formally ended at 4:15. In the winter months, darkness will blanket the sky throughout this entire period of meditation and *lectio*. At the height of summer, however, the rising sun measures off the prayerful progression toward Lauds. In either case, the monk, steeped in prayer and enveloped in the arms of God, as the hood of his robe represents, seeks to fulfill what Saint John Cassian said was the role of all monks: "The whole purpose of the monk and indeed the perfection of his heart amount to this—total and uninterrupted dedication to prayer."[2]

After Vigils is complete, I like to remain sitting in choir for a half hour of meditation. Many of the monks do the same. After my meditation I return to my room. Here, with the hood of my smock pulled up over my head, I feel the warm embrace of God as I lose myself in an hour of *lectio*. That embrace continues when I sit for another half hour of meditation following my *lectio*.

Yes, sleep is sometimes a problem. At other times, sleep is the farthest thing from my mind. On those occasions when I am attacked by drowsiness, I simply pace the room for a few moments, or step into the small kitchen across the hall and make myself a cup of hot chocolate.

Vigils is about waiting, waiting for Jesus. In the choir and in our rooms we await the Master in prayer and psalms.

NOTES

[1] André Louf, *The Cistercian Way* (Kalamazoo, Mich.: Cistercian Publications, 1983), pp. 51-52.

[2] Saint John Cassian, *Conferences*, trans. Colm Luibheid (Mahwah, N.J.: Paulist Press, 1985), p. 101.

6

Beginnings

I have been baptized twice. The first time was as an infant at what was then Calvary Methodist Church in New Albany, Indiana. Water was poured over my head on April 18, 1954, three months after I was born.

I was twelve years old when I was baptized the second time. Again, it was in New Albany, but this time at the First Baptist Church. On the Sunday prior to this baptism I had come forward at the altar call toward the end of the Sunday morning service to give myself to Christ, to accept Jesus as my "personal Lord and Savior." This surprised my grandmother. I had been sitting with her during this service, and when the routine invitation was given I bolted down the aisle. That surprised her, but it also delighted her. After that service had ended, as many people came forward and congratulated *her* as congratulated me for having given myself to Christ. My grandmother was most impressed.

First Baptist Church, however, was not impressed with my infant baptism. Since I had now firmly and unequivocally given myself to Jesus, I must subsequently be properly baptized—which means being completely submerged.

None of that pouring-water-over-the-forehead-infant-baptism for First Baptist Church! So one week after striding forward at the weekly altar call, I was dunked in the baptismal pool on a Sunday evening by the Reverend McKinny. On the ninth day of October 1966, I became a Baptist.

What made me accept that altar call on the Sunday before my second baptism? The Holy Spirit, of course, cannot be discounted. But the more mundane answer was that it was due to the mission that had been preached several weeks prior to my walking down the aisle.

I cannot recall his name, but a preacher was brought in to instill the fear of God into the young teenagers of the church. This ringer was loud, bombastic and full of hell fire. Obviously, he made a big impression on me. No way was I going to hell.

First Baptist Church became my church long before I answered that altar call. I remember being in the second-grade Sunday School class, which my grandmother taught. I recall singing at the Christmas service. Easter sunrise service was always a treat, for after the service there were doughnuts and sausage and biscuits in the basement of the Sunday School building. When I think of my childhood experience of church, I remember my grandmother, my mother's mother, Nellie Rodgers. When my grandmother died in November of 1998, her funeral was held at First Baptist. The first twenty minutes of her funeral service was simply the organist playing all the old hymns she loved, hymns I had grown up with, too, and love to this day: "In the Garden," "How Great Thou Art," "Amazing Grace," "Nearer My God to Thee," "Shall We Gather at the River."

But I do not remember much else about First Baptist Church. Not long after my baptism there, I grew tired of going to church and Sunday School. My mother tried to get me to go, but I put up a fuss, and after a while she gave up trying. In my late teens, I returned to church. It was not First Baptist, however, to which I returned, but a church about ten blocks down the street—Central Christian Church. Central was, and is, of the Disciples of Christ denomination. It was also the church of one Sara Jacoby whom I had begun dating, and whom I would eventually marry.

7

College and the Floral Shop

Pretentiousness is sometimes the hallmark of the college crowd. Fortunately, most students outgrow this temporary bout of academy-itis and move on, leaving the hardcore to tilt at the windmills of conceit.

I suffered from this affliction. This malady manifested itself in many forms, but it was especially acute in the area of religion. Although I never fell off the cliff into atheism, I did jump feet first into deism. Jesus of Nazareth? An itinerate preacher his followers idealized as God. The Almighty? The unmoved mover of Aristotle, the remote being of the Enlightenment who winds up the clock, slams it down on the table, then walks away, allowing it all to tick away, come what may.

Through my junior year of high school, academics were secondary to athletics, especially swimming. My heroes were James "Doc" Councilman and Mark Spitz. But in 1972, when I enrolled in John Richardson's humanities class in my senior year at New Albany High School, things began to change. Formerly, I lugged Councilman's *The Science of Swimming* along with me on swim meets. Now,

Camus's *The Myth of Sisyphus* and Beckett's *Waiting for Godot* were my reading material on the bus rides to and from those swim meets. Plato blew me away, and Sartre was cool. I mean, who *were* those guys?

In college, at Indiana University, I was an English major and loved it. T. S. Eliot was my poet, and James Joyce was my inspiration. When I took an individual studies course in Joyce under the direction of Dr. Carol Bishop, she assigned me *Dubliners, A Portrait of the Artist as a Young Man* and *Ulysses*—all in one semester. I dove into *Finnegans Wake*, not understanding at all what I was reading, but enjoying the few puns I could understand. I was in heaven. I contributed poems (dreadful ones) to the school literary magazine. I fancied myself one day becoming an English professor, ensconced in a world of ivy and ideas.

What religious faith remained in me I practiced at Central Christian Church. Sara and I sang in the choir, but the real fun was in the youth group. There I jousted with the youth director over issues of Christology and ecclesiology. I also relished poking fun at the fundamentalism of some of my fellow students.

I enjoyed playing the role of the class doubter, and I played it to the hilt. The Apostle "I'll-not believe-it-till-I-see-the-nail-holes-in-his-hands" Thomas was my mentor. One person, however, never backed down from my wisecracks and scornful observations. She willingly engaged me in debate and, furthermore, she seemed to enjoy the match as much as I. That, I liked. Her name was Martha Saunders, and she was the wife of the pastor of Central Christian Church.

I attended college in New Albany from the fall of 1972 to the spring of 1976. Indiana University Southeast is located there, the Southeast campus having moved from nearby Jeffersonville to New Albany in my sophomore year. I lived at home. Sara, a year behind me, lived at home as well.

During those undergraduate days I worked at a floral shop driving the delivery van. Nance Floral Shoppe was, and still is, located at the corner of Eighth and Spring in New Albany, across from the former St. Edward's Hospital where I was born.

During the school year, I worked part time, while during the summer I worked full time. My job at Nance's was the most fun job I have ever had, period. My job was to deliver flowers, and my primary route was in the country, outside New Albany. I would load up the van right after lunch, then head off for Sellersburg, Henryville, Charlestown and New Washington. I would not return to the shop until late afternoon, when I would sweep the workroom floor where the women arranged the floral decorations before going home.

Cruising down the highway was fun, and the people I encountered on the job were always interesting. For instance, the older lady with orange hair who would swear on a stack of Bibles that a wild bird was loose in her home and would I please sweep it away? There was Kate who worked at the Sellersburg branch of the floral shop. Kate was left-handed. When she gave me instructions on how to get to a certain house in Sellersburg she would say, "OK, honey"—Kate called everybody "honey"— "you turn *right* when you come to the first stop sign, then turn *left* at the very next street." The problem was when she said *right* she meant *left*, and when she said *left* she meant *right*, so you had to reverse everything she said. It took me a while to catch on to Kate's sense of direction. There were the funeral home cut-ups who liked to play bizarre games with a gun loaded with blanks. One of these games was to burst in on you while you were all alone in the back room where the flowers were actually deposited. You would be in there, alone, bringing in the flowers, when all of a sudden the door would fly open and out would pop one of the funeral home directors brandishing a blank gun and firing away. Or there was the massage parlor up in Clarksville where I delivered the dozen red roses. Most of all, though, I enjoyed being out on the road. I savored the freedom of movement, and I seriously entertained becoming an over-the-road truck driver upon graduation. *Overdrive* magazine was essential reading for me at this time.

But there was another aspect of the job that had a direct impact on my spiritual development. Part of my job was to deliver flowers to Holy Family Catholic Church and St. Mary's Catholic Church in New Albany. Each church received two vases of flowers every Saturday, which I was to place on or near the altars. During my first two years on the job I didn't think much of it: rush into the church, place the flowers where they were supposed to go and get out fast for the next delivery. But in my final two years of college, when I began to doubt my doubt about religion, the weekly trips to these two churches took on greater significance.

What exactly it was that made me doubt my doubt remains a mystery to me. I only know that by the time of my junior year in college, 1975, I began to really listen to what was being said at Central Christian. From the choir I actually began to listen to Reverend Saunders's sermon, not just to find flaws in its logic. Instead of seeking argumentation and conflict at the youth group, I sought enlightenment and peace. Now, this was a gradual process; I did not cease sarcastic quips overnight. But I noticed the change within me and so did Martha Saunders.

Martha Saunders was not only close to the youth group; she had also been my math teacher in junior high school. She taught me general mathematics in the seventh grade and algebra in the ninth at Hazelwood Junior High School. To this day, I can see her standing in front of the math class exhorting us to give mathematics our best effort. "YOUGOTTAWANNA" she would write on the board, "You have got to want to do it," she would say.

Well, I did not "wanna" do math (and my grades reflected that lack of desire) in junior high school, but I did wanna' seek God in my final years of college. When it came to my seeking God, Martha Saunders did not so much debate me as engage me; she did not so much seek to convert me, as to enlighten me. Her manner of enlightenment was so refined and relaxed, with not a hint of confrontation, that I was bowled over by her subdued attack. In essence, I was torpedoed. When engaging with her, I did not seek to score polemical points, but sought really to *know*.

One Sunday afternoon, long after the worship service had ended, I walked into the empty sanctuary of Central. I sat down in the front pew. Up and to my right was a stained glass window depicting Jesus standing at the door of a house. He is knocking on the door, and his head is tilted as if he is listening for a response from within. The message of the stained glass is clear. I recall sitting in that pew and wondering why I could not hear Jesus knocking at *my* door. I would gladly open the door, I said to the window, if you would only knock on the door! I felt angry and resentful that everyone in the youth group at Central seemed to have heard Jesus knock on their doors, but Jesus had not, or so it seemed, knocked at mine.

Of course, Jesus was knocking at the door, but I was filled with too much self-pity and arrogance to hear it. I *saw* him knocking, however, at those two churches where I delivered flowers every Saturday, Holy Family and St. Mary's. Now I began to linger in those churches when I delivered the flowers. Nobody was ever there when I delivered the flowers, so my looking around was not disturbing anyone. I was particularly intrigued with St. Mary's. Having been raised as a Baptist, I was unaccustomed to such an ornate church. So, after placing the flowers in their usual place, I began sitting in the pews and looking around. Not only did St. Mary's not look like First Baptist, it bore no resemblance to Central Christian Church, either. Why all those flickering candles? What were those fourteen figures lining the walls of the church, each one numbered? Why those dishes of water at the doors? Why was there a railing crossing the width of the church near the front? What was in that little gold box on the altar against the back wall? And what was with those statues? But as strongly as I was attracted to the sights of the church, I was more strongly attracted by its smell. St. Mary's and Holy Family smelled *holy*. Not that First Baptist or Central Christian smelled *unholy* or holy or anything else. But upon entering St. Mary's and Holy Family each Saturday, it was the smell of the church I noticed first, not its sights. Those sights and smells combined to tell me that I was entering someplace different. Going in and out of Central Christian Sunday after Sunday was no different than going in and out of the local supermarket. When I stepped into St. Mary's and Holy Family Saturday after Saturday, however, I felt I was crossing over from the secular into the divine.

Now I admit that the difference in my experience of St. Mary's and Holy Family from my experience of other churches could simply have been a classic case of "familiarity breeds contempt"; Central was old hat to me, while St. Mary's and Holy Family were new and exotic. My awe of St. Mary's and Holy Family could have been due to the fact that they were just new and different experiences. Had I been raised Catholic and walked into First Baptist or

Central for the first time as a young adult, my reaction might well have been the same. Perhaps. Nevertheless, my experience at St. Mary's and Holy Family was genuine, and the reality of the situation was that I was truly touched by what I saw and smelled, and the experience there was radically different from anything I had experienced at Central or First Baptist.

I brought questions back to the floral shop. Many of the women who worked at the shop were Catholic, and I peppered them with questions. Their answers led to more questions. One day, one of the ladies at the shop brought me a newspaper. It was called *Our Sunday Visitor*. I took it home and devoured it. Reading it was like being bombarded with a new language, words I had never encountered: *liturgy, sacristy, sacramentary, lectionary, thurible*. The next day I asked my coworker how I could get more copies of the paper. She told me that issues were often stashed in the foyers of churches, free for the taking. The following Saturday I headed to the foyer of St. Mary and Holy Family churches and, sure enough, I found different issues of *Our Sunday Visitor*. From that day until my last day of work at the shop, I picked up a copy of that paper every Saturday.

So, on that Sunday as I was sitting in the empty sanctuary of Central Christian Church looking up at the stained glass window depicting Jesus knocking at the door, these thoughts of St. Mary's and Holy Family and *Our Sunday Visitor* were all racing through my head. And as I sat there thinking all these thoughts, I realized I needed to make a decision.

The decision I had to make was whether or not to be Christian. Though I was baptized, though I was singing in a church choir, though I was attending a Sunday School youth group, I did not consider myself Christian. How could I if I had scoffed at the divinity of Jesus of Nazareth?

In my mind I had to start over, and that meant that I had to publicly profess my faith in Jesus as the Christ.

I knew such a public profession would be embarrassing. For one thing, in the eyes of Central Christian Church I already was Christian; the congregation saw me every Sunday in the choir and in the youth group. Second, I was twenty years old, and public professions of faith were usually the domain of early adolescents. Third, to make this profession I would have to stand up and leave the choir while it was singing the song of invitation. Furthermore, the choir was not only seated up front in full view of the congregation, it was also seated in an area elevated higher than the seated congregation. The instant I stood up I would be tagged. No, this would in no way be similar to the time I bolted down the aisle at First Baptist Church just eight years earlier.

However, it would be a more sincere profession. The impediment of fear ("And so I ask you, are you saved!? Do you want to spend all eternity in hell?!!!") would be gone. This profession would be made in freedom.

So, on the Sunday morning following my talk with the stained glass window, I made my move. When Reverend Saunders gave the invitation for profession of faith, I stood up and walked through the choir, my choir robe rustling against legs and chairs. I walked down the steps by the pulpit, and took a seat in the front row of pews. The choir was belting out a hymn, the title of which I have long ago forgotten. I'm sure I was red-faced, and I recall feeling hot, but no sooner had I sat down than someone else joined me. It was Martha Saunders. While the choir was still singing, she whispered into my ear, "You're a believer once again, aren't you?" I nodded my head. When the hymn was over, Reverend Saunders had me stand, and he welcomed me to the membership of Central Christian Church. You see, he and others believed I had come forward simply to transfer my church membership to Central Christian. Only God, Sara and Martha Saunders knew my true motivation.

I had no visions nor did I hear any angelic hallelujahs when I made my second profession of faith. On that Sunday when I had spoken to the stained glass window, when I had decided to make yet a second profession of faith, I heard no voices, felt no pat on the back, nor felt any assurance from God about the decision. I was certain, however, that the decision was the correct one.

I knew something else, too. I knew I could not go back to the status quo. I knew I could not go back to the same church, same Sunday School, same teachers. I knew I could not return to all that and pretend nothing had changed. For something had changed: God had changed me. God had set me in a new direction. The only trouble was, I did not know which direction God was pointing me.

What I did know was that I was forever Christian. But in what form would this Christianity express itself? I decided to start over.

8

Bloomington

Anna Mae Cardin was born Anna Mae Roth in 1908, the oldest of six. When she married my grandfather in January of 1926, she became Ann Plaiss and gave birth to five children in five years: Edith, Betty, Barbara, George (my father, nicknamed Bud) and Robert. Five in five, as my dad used to say. After she and my grandfather divorced, she married Harold Cardin and bore one child, my Aunt Jennifer.

When I think of my Grandma, I think of Christmas Eve. Every year we gathered at her house on Christmas Eve. My father's four sisters and one brother, their families, my parents and brothers all squeezed into her modest home behind Providence High School in Clarksville. When I was quite small these gatherings were held in her front living room, though a large contingent always spilled over into the kitchen. Later, a larger family room was built onto the back of the house behind the kitchen, and after the completion of that addition the Christmas Eve bash was always held there.

And a bash it was. We would arrive about seven o'clock in the evening, and immediately we would fall into singing, arguing and telling stories. Grandma always had cookies, fudge and divinity stashed about the room, and the refrigerator was stocked with ample beer and soft drinks. Cigarette smoke grew so thick that the door had to be opened to vent the room. Wrapping paper was strewn all over the floor, and you could not walk from one place to another without tripping over someone or something.

Politics and sports were the major topics of argument. Wit was king in these slugfests, not logic. The object was not so much to win the debate as it was to score the point. The prize went to the one with the quickest comeback, the cutest quip or the sharpest dig. Hence, the smart aleck ruled. It also helped to be especially *loud* when driving home your point.

Everybody sang. Quality of voice was incidental, though there were enough good voices to carry most songs. Seasonal or secular, the type of song made no difference. We sang anything from "Silent Night" to "Please Don't Talk about Me When I'm Gone." Barbershop harmony was the goal, and more often than not it was attained. When it was not, however, the song would collapse in a heap of discordance that would grate the ears of a sow. Knowledge of the lyrics to these songs was optional, for the goal was to "ring the chord." When a lyric escaped one's mind, any word or group of words would do, as long as it fit into the rhythm of the song.

In the middle of all this chaos sat my grandmother. I sensed she was amused by the uproar that descended upon her house every Christmas Eve. Rarely did she sing, but now and then she would interject a zinger into an argument that would either totally baffle the combatants or nail the issue to the wall. She alone among the adults received gifts, but she always had presents for the little ones beneath the Christmas tree.

As swell a time as everyone had on Christmas Eve, all left her house by ten o'clock. Grandma was Catholic, and she attended Midnight Mass. She needed to get ready in order to leave early enough to get a good seat at church.

One Christmas Eve my father and his sisters and brother chipped in and gave their mother a very expensive rosary. She was very moved by the gift, and she wept. I was puzzled by her reaction. What was it that had made her weep? The fact that her children had given her an expensive gift? The fact that her children had given her a gift *at all?* Could it have been the rosary itself, or because the rosary was so beautiful and expensive? Who knows? I remember her holding it so delicately and reverently, and how she passed it around for others to see and hold. The evening ended as it always did, in a hail of songs both seasonal and secular, around ten o'clock. By the time we left that night, I had completely forgotten about the rosary and her emotional reaction upon receiving it.

Forgotten about it, that is, until years later when I was delivering flowers and gawking at churches, years later when I was ready to make a move in my spiritual life. Then that memory of my grandmother receiving her rosary came rushing back to me; then I recalled the reason *why* we always had to leave her house by ten. By the time I was pondering my move to Catholicism, however, I was not interested in what caused her to weep upon receiving that rosary; I was intrigued by the gift itself. I was not concerned with the reasons for leaving her house at ten o'clock on Christmas Eve; I was interested in where she was going. Though my grandmother had never spoken a word to me about religion in general or Catholicism in particular, her example was an inspiration to me.

By the fall of 1975, I was in my senior year of college at Indiana University Southeast in New Albany, and my curiosity about Catholicism had grown beyond my just sitting in St. Mary and Holy Family churches. It had also deepened beyond what *Our Sunday Visitor* could provide. I needed more information. It was at this time that the *Catholic Encyclopedia* became my friend.

I would sit in the library at school and read entry after entry on topics: Mass, transubstantiation, the pope, Mary, religious orders and hundreds of other things that caught my eye as I browsed through the encyclopedia. The pictures there were important, as well. I was most curious about vestments, altars and church architecture. The more I read, and the more I explored St. Mary and Holy Family, the more I realized the change that was coming over me. Catholicism was becoming more and more inviting.

While Catholicism was becoming more inviting, Central was growing more troublesome. My reading sparked questions. Why did the Old Testament of the Protestant Bible differ from the Old Testament of the Catholic Bible? Since the Christian Bible was already intact, upon whose authority was the decision made to exclude those books? From whence did this authority derive? If the Protestant churches had the authority to remove books from the Old Testament, did it follow that they had the authority to add or delete books from the New Testament as well? If they had the authority, from whence did it come? If they did not, *why* did they not, given the ability they had to drop books from the Old Testament? Finally, in the sixth chapter of John, was Jesus speaking literally or figuratively when he spoke of the Bread of Life? If he were speaking figuratively, why did Jesus *not* call back those disciples who walked away from him because they found his words about the Bread of Life "hard to endure," and why did he not reassure these disciples that his speech was figurative? If Jesus was being literal in the sixth chapter of John when he spoke of the Bread of Life, why was Central telling me that the words were figurative?

No longer was Jesus of Nazareth the stumbling block; I had passed that hurdle. The difficulty now was the church, and specifically the question of authority as it related to the church. The answers I received from Central no longer rang true. In fact, they seemed to drop with a thud.

The question eventually came to me: why limit myself to Protestantism? I was making a new start in the faith. I wanted to remain true to that faith. Why return to that form of Christianity that had fomented seeds of discontent within me in the first place? Why return to a form of Christianity that seemed either unwilling to answer my questions, or unable to do so? Why not seek a new expression of Christianity to correspond with my fresh start in the faith? Just because I was born into a nominally Protestant family did not mean I had to remain there.

I saw Christianity as divided up into three broad groups: Catholicism, Orthodoxy and Protestantism. I was familiar with the latter. Orthodoxy was intriguing and mysterious, but it had two strikes against it, both mundane. One, I knew absolutely no person who was Orthodox. Two, there were no Orthodox churches around. Louisville had some, but they were too far away for me to attend. Catholicism was easy at hand, and I knew plenty of Catholics, one of whom was my grandmother.

In the summer of 1976, during dinner with my parents, I asked them, "Would it bother you if I joined the Catholic Church?"

Not at all, came the reply both from my mother and father. However, my father immediately shot back with, "You know they believe the pope is infallible."

"You believe that?" my mother asked.

Now the infallibility of the pope was something I had

looked up in the *Catholic Encyclopedia*, and I knew it had something to do with whatever *ex cathedra* was, but I really did not know much about the dogma. So I just brushed off their questions with, "I'm comfortable with it."

But there was a problem. Sara and I were to be married in December of 1976. I did not believe it would be fair to her for me to switch denominations less than six months prior to our marriage. She and I agreed that after the wedding when we would be living in Bloomington would be the more appropriate time for me to seek entrance into the Catholic Church.

Sara and I married on December 26, 1976, at Central Christian Church in New Albany. Less than a month later, in mid January of 1977, I was taking instruction to be received into the Catholic Church. Sara supported me completely in this venture. Thirteen years later Sara was received into the Catholic Church at Easter Vigil.

In the late summer of 1976, Sara and I both transferred to the main campus of Indiana University in Bloomington. I had received a bachelor's degree in English the previous spring at the Southeast campus and was entering graduate school on the Bloomington campus. Sara was completing her final year of undergraduate school before applying for entrance into the Indiana University dental school. Sara lived in Moffet Hall, and I was housed in Foley. Our dormitories were less than a hundred yards apart.

There were two Catholic churches in Bloomington at the time Sara and I were living there. St. Charles Borromeo was located on Third Street down the road from the College Mall, while St. Paul was located on the other end of the campus on Seventeenth Street. St. Paul also housed the Newman Center. I selected St. Charles Borremeo as the church where I would receive my Catholic instruction for one simple reason: it looked like what I at the time thought a Catholic church should look like. I did not talk to any of the priests at either parish prior to making my decision on which church in which to receive instruction. Nor did I approach any of the parishioners of either parish to elicit their help in making my decision. After stopping by both churches, looking around in both and saying a prayer, I simply called the number for St. Charles in November of 1976. I was told an instructional class would be starting in January of 1977. In hindsight, I find my criteria for selection both crude and inadequate, but such was my state of mind at the time. God could only work with what he had.

I began attending Sunday Mass during that fall of 1976. Except for the wedding Mass of my cousin, I had never attended a Mass. I made all the usual mistakes many non-Catholics make when attending Mass for the first time: I genuflected on the left knee instead of the right. I made the Sign of the Cross the wrong way. I tacked on a phrase at the end of the Our Father ("...for thine is the Kingdom..."). I felt as though I were wearing a scarlet P on my chest; I was certain everyone there *knew* I was an outsider, a Protestant.

What really interested me about Mass was Communion. At both First Baptist and Central Christian, the tiny communion cups and the sliver of bread were brought to the assembly and passed down the pews, each person taking an individual cup or fragment of bread. At First Baptist, all this was done monthly. At Central Christian, it was done weekly. In both places, however, the assembly always remained seated in the pews and Communion was brought to them. From the vantage point of the back pews at St. Charles, however, I carefully observed how the assembly, row by row, walked forward and received Communion from the priest standing at the steps of the sanctuary. What also intrigued me was that Communion was obviously the high point of the Mass, whereas at First Baptist and at Central

Christian, the sermon was certainly the apex of the Sunday service. That difference made a very deep impression upon me.

I did not attend Mass every Sunday at St. Charles, however. Sometimes I walked down to the Disciples of Christ church for Sunday services. I usually did this in order to receive Communion. But as January 1977 drew closer, I attended the Disciples church less often, and after I began instruction at St. Charles, I stopped going to the Disciples church altogether.

The priest's name was Father Charles Fischer, and he was the assistant pastor at St. Charles. He was the first priest I had ever seen with a beard. Once a week a small group of us, no more than ten, met with him in the parish school to receive instruction in order to be received into the Catholic Church. Father Chuck, as he wished to be called, was young. In January of 1977, when I started taking instruction, he could not have been more than a few years out of seminary. He possessed a great singing voice, and he frequently chanted the Eucharistic Prayer during Mass. Our little class met in the parish school, across the parking lot from the church. Our textbook was *Christ Among Us* by Anthony J. Wilhelm. [1]

The winter of 1977 was unusually cold. The Ohio River froze over, grinding barge traffic to a halt. People even tried walking back and forth between Indiana and Kentucky on the icy river. Fortunately, my parents were gracious enough to give Sara and me a car—a gold 1968 Ford Galaxy. That made traveling to and from St. Charles much more pleasant.

I was the only man in the group. All the young women in the group were entering the church because they were to be married to Catholic men. Our hour-long weekly classes basically followed the Wilhelm book chapter by chapter.

Some weeks we covered only one chapter, while other weeks we plowed through several. There were no grand discussions among the group. Most of my questions centered around the Eucharist.

As Easter approached, Father Chuck began speaking of the rite of penance—confession. If there was one thing I was not looking forward to about being Catholic, it was confession. The mere thought of telling my sins to a priest struck me with fear and dread. Embarrassment big time! Father Chuck did a good job, however, preparing us, and when the time came for our first confession I was . . . full of fear and dread. But once I was in the confessional, face to face with him, the fear and dread evaporated. The experience was not one of retribution, but of healing. I emerged feeling a weight had been lifted from my shoulders and, yes, relief that it was over.

The time between January and Easter seemed to fly by. Sara and I were now living in married housing on campus. After attending my instructional class, I would return to our efficiency apartment all excited. I would discuss (and perhaps bore) Sara with all that we had studied in class, and I would bring up all the questions I had thought of during the short drive home. I taught myself the prayers to the rosary (though I did not buy the beads until we later moved to Indianapolis), and I memorized the responses for Mass.

One memorable event during this time was an evening Mass at St. Charles celebrated by a group of monks from St. Meinrad Archabbey in Southwestern Indiana. The whole Mass was celebrated in Latin, and the monks sang it in Gregorian chant. The idea was to celebrate the Mass as it would have been celebrated in the Middle Ages. The church that evening was packed, and many professors from the classics department of the university attended. I was bowled over by the chant, hearing it live for the first time.

The chant was pure euphony. That Mass was also the first time I encountered incense. The Gregorian chant coupled with the sweet smell of incense lifted me to heights I had never experienced before. This was light years beyond anything I had known at First Baptist or Central Christian. That evening at St. Charles I was anointed; I sensed the divine; I felt at home.

As Easter approached, Father Chuck told us of our need for a sponsor for reception of the sacrament of confirmation that would be conferred upon us at the Easter Mass. This sponsor, of course, had to be Catholic. The trouble was that I did not know any Catholics who lived in the Bloomington area. All the Catholics I knew personally, and whom I would be comfortable asking to sponsor me, lived in New Albany. But even they were either non-practicing Catholics or twice-a-year Catholics. Still another problem lay in the fact that the Easter Mass during which I would be received into the Catholic Church would be held at six o'clock in the morning. So, even if I could round up somebody from New Albany to be my sponsor, that person would either have to come up to Bloomington and spend Saturday night in a hotel, or leave New Albany very early on Sunday morning. Either alternative involved time, expense and inconvenience. The solution to my problem came with Louann, Sara's sister. Louann was living on the Indiana University campus, too, and her roommate, a Catholic, agreed to be my sponsor. Her name was Molly Mills.

Easter 1977 fell on April 10. Though the day would turn sunny and warm, it began cloudy and cold. Mass began promptly at 6:00 A.M. Among those in attendance were Sara and her two sisters, Louann and Laura, and their parents, Laird and Sue Jacoby. Laird, Sue and Laura had driven up from New Albany that morning. The Mass was two hours long. When it was time for me to receive the sacrament of confirmation I stood with the other candidates. Molly stood behind me and placed her right hand on my right shoulder. Father Robert Borchortmeyer, the pastor of St. Charles, walked down the line of candidates. He anointed me with oil. "Peace be with you," he said. "And also with you," I replied. But as much as I had looked forward to receiving confirmation, it was Holy Communion that I was longing for. No ambiguity, no symbolism, but the Body and Blood of the Lord! "The Body of Christ," said Father Borchortmeyer, as I later approached him for my First Holy Communion.

"Amen," I said.

And it was complete.

The next day, Monday, I stopped by St. Charles for the five o'clock evening Mass. With only a handful of us present, Father Chuck invited the assembly forward to stand around the altar after the prayers of intercession. When it came time for reception of Holy Communion, we received the chalice as well as the Host. For me, reception of the chalice was the exclamation point to my first Holy Communion.

Two weeks later I received a small package from my grandmother Cardin. Days before Easter I had written her telling her about my upcoming reception into the Catholic Church. Now, she had sent me a gift celebrating that reception. It was a silver four-way medal necklace. I wear it always.

NOTE

[1] Anthony J. Wilhelm, *Christ Among Us: A Modern Presentation of the Catholic Faith for Adults*, 6th Revised Edition (San Francisco: HarperSanFrancisco, 1996).

9

Lauds and Vespers

Morning prayer and evening prayer—Lauds and Vespers—are the "two hinges on which the daily office turns."[1] They are the two most important Offices of the day, and even if some of the community cannot be present in choir at all of the Offices, they make an extra effort to be present at Lauds and Vespers.

The importance of morning and evening praise stretches back to the time of the Old Testament.

> Why emphasize morning and evening as special times of prayer? The ancient prescription found in the law of the Old Testament, viz., sacrifice of a lamb twice a day (Ex 29:38–39) and the daily twofold offering of incense (Ex 30:6–8), was carried over into the early church which now sanctified these two times with prayer. [2]

In the early church, morning and evening prayer, not daily Mass, was the backbone of the average Christian's day. The author of the Apostolic Constitutions around the year A.D. 380 wrote, "When you instruct the people, O Bishop, command and exhort them to make it a practice to come *daily* to the church *in the morning and in the evening. . .*

singing and praying in the Lord's house, in the morning saying Psalm 62 and in the evening Psalm 140" (emphasis added). Over the centuries daily Eucharist gradually replaced daily morning and evening prayer for the average Christian. With this gradual emphasis on daily Eucharist, morning and evening prayer became the domain almost exclusively of monks and clergy.

Coming some two hours after Vigils, Lauds has a strikingly different tone than that of Vigils. Whereas the theme of Vigils is waiting and watching, the theme of Lauds is praise. And if the symbol of Vigils is darkness, the symbol of Lauds is light. This is so even when Lauds is prayed in the darkness of the winter months. Lauds has a more cheerful tone. Depending on the time of year, the sun has just inched its way over the horizon when Lauds cranks up, and all the promises and concerns of the day lie ahead.

Both Lauds and Vespers each have a Gospel canticle that is peculiar to it. Both canticles come from the Gospel of Luke, and those canticles are *always* a part of their respective Hours. At Lauds that canticle is the Benedictus, the song of Zechariah (Luke 1:68–79); at Vespers that canticle is the Magnificat, the song of Mary (Luke 1:46–55).

Vespers is the Hour of thanksgiving. The community looks back upon the day and gives thanks to God for blessings and graces. The sun is setting and night approaches (or may already have fallen, depending upon the time of year) as Vespers is sung, and the community prepares to settle in for the night.

At New Melleray, Lauds is at 6:30 A.M. Mass immediately follows Lauds during the week, but on Sundays, Mass is at 10:30. Vespers at New Melleray is at 5:30 P.M. The guest area is usually crowded for both Lauds and Vespers.

When I came down for Lauds on this particular morning, Matt was already in his place. I stepped past him and into the stall immediately to his left. As I knelt down upon the floor at my stall, I flashed forward to everything I wanted to accomplish on this day that lay ahead of me. I wanted a good day of prayer. I wanted to study Saint John Cassian's ninth Conference. I wanted to feel closer to God. I wondered what afternoon work I would be assigned; I hoped it would be outside.

As I was rattling through my itinerary, making my list and checking it twice, I was making the mistake of many a monk. I was not properly aware of the moment. I was not doing what I was supposed to be doing at that given moment in time. I was supposed to be preparing my soul and mind for prayer by calming myself, by focusing on the upcoming morning praise. Instead, I was anxious about things and events whose time had not yet come. I was not praying, but planning, and the moment demanded prayer.

I shook my head to clear my thoughts. I took some deep breaths. I decided that I could pray better if my knees and back didn't hurt so much, so I pulled down the wooden seat in my stall and sat down. I tried to empty my mind of thoughts and cares, to simply rest in God.

The first bell rang. Monks are called to choir by the chime of bells. For each Office there are two bells. The first bell rings five minutes before the Office commences. One Monastic Center wag used to refer to the first bell as a warning bell. I prefer to view it as a call to worship. Whatever the moniker, the first bell means Office is minutes away. When the second bell has rung five minutes later, the Office begins.

With the ringing of the first bell the lights snapped on. I, and those around me, stood up. Immediately, we began finding the proper places in the psalter, antiphonary and hymnal. I was sure of the proper psalms and hymn, but the antiphonary was dealing me fits. I could not for the life of me find the proper place in it, and without finding the proper place, I would not know the proper antiphons attached to the psalms, and without knowing the proper antiphons that were attached to the proper psalms, I would not be able to sing them, and when the guys around me saw that I wasn't singing, they would know I was an idiot. Drat! I looked to my right at Matt. He was fumbling through the antiphonary as well. He looked over at me looking at him, and his facial expression said, "I'm lost, too." I shot a glance down the choir to my left. Three stalls down, one of the brothers was expertly finding his place in the books. I was about to step down to him and ask for assistance, when I saw a welcome sight. St. Louis Paul had entered the church, and he was making his bow before the altar.

Paul, who had entered the community nearly a year ago, walked swiftly down the choir, his novice robes billowing. He slipped past me and Matt, and took his place immediately to Matt's right. Paul quickly flipped through the pages of the books, setting them at the proper places. He looked over at Matt who shrugged his shoulders and nodded his head toward the books. Paul saw the problem and set the antiphonary to the proper page. I followed suit by looking at Matt's book.

With that crisis over, we turned in our stalls and faced the altar. In Cistercian houses it is customary to begin the Office facing the altar. I glanced out the window immediately to my left. Day was finally beginning to dawn. I could make out, now, the dew on the grass. I saw birds dart in and out of bushes. Bill entered the church and made his bow before the altar. Bill, like Paul, had also recently entered the community. He, too, was in his novice robes. He moved past me and Matt and took his place in choir next to Paul.

The second bell rang, and everyone seemed to

straighten up, seemed to stand a little taller. The organ sounded the tone, and the cantor jumped on it.

"O God, come to my assistance," he chanted.

"O Lord, make haste to help me," we responded. And with that we all turned in our stalls to face the center of the church, the two choirs facing one another. In a deep bow we continued chanting, "Glory be to the Father, and to the Son, and to the Holy Spirit, both now and forever." Standing up from the bow we continued, "As it was in the beginning is now and ever shall be, world without end. Amen."

The remaining Offices throughout the day would begin in like manner.

NOTES

[1] *Constitution on the Sacred Liturgy*, no. 89a, *Vatican Council II: The Conciliar and Post Conciliar Documents*, general ed. Austin Flannery, O.P. (Northport, N.Y.: Costello Publishing Co., 1987), p. 25.

[2] Juan Maetos, "The Morning and Evening Office," *Worship* 42 (1968), p. 32.

10

Faith

*F*aith is not a feeling. Faith may very well produce intense feelings, but that is not faith. Faith is a gift from God in the form of a decision to love, trust and follow God. Faith is blind, but based on love. The object of faith is unseen, but anchored in reason and hope.

Faith is a journey, but a journey that is not linear, for faith is not geometry. The journey is not from point A to point B, but an exploration of the depths of the human heart to discover the image of God, peel away the sin that has tarnished the image, confront it, rest there and ultimately transcend the self. In this journey one can never dig too deeply, nor can one ever reach the bottom, for love, on which faith is based, is unfathomable.

The journey may seemingly veer off the "path." This is an illusion. On the journey of faith, one can never veer off the path, for the path includes all those sins and moments of doubt we mistakenly believe push us off the path. On the journey of faith, one is always on the path. The only way to be off the path is not to be on the journey in the first place. The end of the journey can never be foreseen. For it to be otherwise would not be faith, but knowledge. God does not ask for our knowledge; God asks for our faith. Time cannot confine faith. It is never too soon nor too late to embrace faith—just ask Luke's thief on the cross (see Luke 23:39-43).

Faith may wane, but most likely it is fervor that wanes, and the two are not the same. The zeal of freshly found faith is white hot, but when plunged into the waters of life . . . well, routine and familiarity quickly cool zeal. What remains is faith shorn of pretense, sentimentality or dogma, and the soul stands naked before God, who asks the question, "What will it be?" And the universe hangs in the balance, for faith is about answering that question. The book of Sirach puts it this way:

> Before man are life and death, whichever he
> chooses shall be given him. (Sirach 15:17)

Upon answering the question, the soul walks toward God through a vast darkness. Without the crutch of creed or church, the soul gropes blindly for God, who has been eagerly awaiting it. The soul is naked and entirely alone, save for God, and it is in this that the soul must place its faith: God is always with us.

Faith cannot be generated, only accepted. Attempts to foster faith by pious thoughts, lengthy prayers or increased church attendance are doomed to failure. One cannot impose oneself on God, nor can one purchase God's favor. Clamping down and vowing through clinched teeth, "I will have faith!" will not work. Faith is openness to God, not demands upon him.

> They who possess the joy of the Lord may preach it and
> commend it to those who do not possess it. They may
> advise them how to seek it and tell them a way to recover

it; and sometimes even, if grace is present, the will may be moved and desire excited. But this joy is tasted only by him into whom it pours itself. No one ascends this summit unless it bends down to him; no one feels this good unless it conforms him to itself; no one lives by this life unless it imparts itself to him.[1]

Faith is not intellectual assent to creeds or dogmas. Creeds and dogmas flow from faith. Abraham did not climb the mountain to follow Torah, but to follow God. Torah came later. Peter did not walk across water to embrace creed, but to embrace Jesus. Faith is fixed upon Jesus. Faith always precedes creed. Creeds and dogmas are important, for they point the way to Jesus, but they are not the Way. Only Jesus is "the Way." Some believe that the sign of the true Christian is the degree to which he or she adheres to doctrinal purity. They believe Saint Paul's great song of love in 1 Corinthians 13:13 reads, "So faith, hope, the magisterium remain, these three; but the greatest of these is the magisterium." Such belief confuses the way for the Way. Faith reduced to rules, codes and rubrics is not faith, but legalism. Legalism is idolatry.

Faith is aided by image. That image is not something ethereal or esoteric; something with which we cannot identify or something we cannot imagine. No, the image walked this earth as a human being and was named Jesus of Nazareth. All the rules, codes and rubrics of the church point the Christian in the direction where that image can be found.

> Know yourself, then, to be my image; thus you can know me, whose image you are, and you will find me within you. If you are with me in your soul, there I will repose with you; and then I will feed you. . . .
>
> Be wholly present to yourself, therefore, and employ yourself wholly in knowing yourself and knowing whose

image you are, and likewise in discerning and understanding what you are and what you can do in him whose image you are.[2]

The image is found within the individual (Genesis 1:27, 2:7; Luke 17:21). The task of the Christian is to discover, encounter and love the image that resides within him or her. Having done so, the Christian transcends the self, enabling him or her to fulfill the law of God: love God, love neighbor and love as Jesus loves—unconditionally.

To recapture the image of God is to be made holy by God. Thus, we strive not to be good, but to be holy (Leviticus 19:2; 1 Peter 1:16). A pagan can be good. The Christian aspires to be holy. One is holy when shrouded in the image of God. One of the early church Fathers, Saint Gregory of Nyssa (c. 335–c. 395) wrote:

> Blessedness does not lie in knowing something about God, but rather in possessing God within oneself . . . you will find what you seek within yourself, provided you return to the beauty and grace of that image which was originally placed in you.[3]

Many traditionalist Christians are wary of the idea of finding God within the self. Though this skepticism is unwarranted, it is understandable. Seeking God within the depths of oneself smacks of New Age. The Christian, however, does not worship the self; the self is renewed through Christ whose image was initially placed within the self at Creation. Furthermore, while the Christian may delve to the image that resides within, the Christian does not remain there. Rather, the Christian, with the grace of God, transcends his or herself in order to love God and neighbor. Merton put it this way:

> . . . to know ourselves is the basis of all our meditation and our prayer, not in the sense that we are the ultimate end of

all our investigations (God preserve us from such a doom), but we come to know God through knowing his image which is implanted in the depth and center and in the very substance of our souls. [4]

By loving God, by being totally consumed by God, the self disappears into union with God. Not that the self becomes God, but that the self can no longer be known apart from God, cannot even be seen apart from God.

Love is the response to the encounter with the image. What bridegroom does not feel pangs of love upon seeing his bride? What bride upon seeing her bridegroom does not have passion for him? The encounter between God and his image is likewise. It is love. We cannot see God face to face, nor can our finite minds contain the infinite God. We can, however, know God by loving God. Again, theologian, mystic and Benedictine abbot, William of Saint-Thierry (c. 1085–1148):

> For love of God itself is knowledge of him; unless he is loved, he is not known, and unless he is known, he is not loved. He is known only insofar as he is loved, and he is loved only insofar as he is known. [5]

Faith, then, is love of God. Faith is not love of rules about God. It is not mere happenstance that love is the great denominator. Jesus said that to inherit everlasting life one must love—love God and neighbor (Luke 10:25–28), and to love others as he loves us (John 15:12). That's it. That is all that matters. John the Evangelist whittled all theology down to a simple equation: "God is love" (1 John 4:8,16). If love is the very definition of God, and not simply an attribute, then love trumps everything, for God trumps everything. Paul flat out champions the primacy of love: "So faith, hope, love remain, these three; but the greatest of these is love" (1 Corinthians 13:13).

If the object of love is God, then union with God is faith. Just as the depth of the union between husband and wife can never be exhausted, so the union of one to God in love can never be exhausted. Love for God, unity with God, can always grow stronger, run deeper, burn brighter. William of Saint-Thierry:

> No longer does it ["unity of spirit" with God] merely desire what God desires, not only does it love him, but it is perfect in its love, so that it can will only what God wills.[6]

Humanity cannot be what it was created to be without it loving God. Abraham Heschel, scholar, author, activist and theologian, wrote:

> Man treats himself as if he were created in the likeness of a machine rather than in the likeness of God. The body is his god, and its needs are his prophets. Having lost his awareness of his sacred image, he became deaf to the meaning: to live in a way which is compatible with his image.[7]

We can only love God, moreover, because God loved us first. Faith and love are inseparable; that is what the fifteenth chapter of Luke's Gospel is all about.

It is sometimes said of a movie that "it was so bad, it was good!" Faith is the same way: it is so *simple* it is hard. All one need do is accept it. Yet we continually categorize it, codify it. We do so because we believe that something so wonderful and grand can only come in a package of gold and silk, can only be approached through arcane systems of thought. We complicate that which is simple. The Magi before the Infant is a perfect illustration. The Magi bring gifts fit for a king, yet the King presents himself as a helpless infant. The Magi's gifts are rare and expensive commodities, but the Lord asks only to be loved, loved as one would love an infant, and such love is inexpensive and available to all.

The journey of faith requires a lifetime. No matter if one lives one hundred years or half that or even half of that, one is always *becoming* in faith, one never *arrives*. This is so *not* because humanity is stupid. It is so because faith is love for God, and the depths of God can never be fathomed and the limits of love can never be reached. Therefore, faith can never be complete, for love can always grow. Faith is a mysterious and sometimes frustrating journey, but all that is ever asked of us is that "if today you hear his voice, harden not your hearts."

NOTES

1 William of Saint-Thierry, *Exposition on the Song of Songs* (Kalamazoo, Mich.: Cistercian Publications, 19), p. 162.

2 *Ibid.*, pp. 51, 53.

3 Gregory of Nyssa, quoted in *The Liturgy of the Hours*, vol. 3 (New York: Catholic Book Publishing, Co., 1976), pp. 413-414.

4 Thomas Merton, "Blessed William of Saint-Thierry: Monk of Signy," *Cistercian Studies Quarterly* 35 (2000), p. 8.

5 William of Saint-Thierry, *Exposition on the Song of Songs*, p. 64.

6 William of Saint-Thierry, *Golden Epistle* (Kalamazoo, Mich.: Cistercian Publications, 1971), p. 94.

7 Abraham Joshua Heschel, *The Insecurity of Freedom* (Philadelphia: Jewish Publication Society of America, 1966), p. 12.

11

Prayer

Prayer is the language of faith. Faith is the love we have for God, and prayer is the expression of that love. As with any language, the language of prayer must be learned. One might protest by saying that true prayer "comes from the heart" and should be "spontaneous." Certainly, prayer often wells up spontaneously from the heart, and that is surely good. However, to consign prayer only to the level of spontaneity is like saying a two-year-old can speak fluently.

In order to learn to pray one must practice. One does not learn to play the piano by listening to piano music. In order to learn to pray one must pray. That may seem self-evident until the time comes when one does not feel like praying. As does the student learning to play the piano, the one learning to pray must practice prayer even when the mood to do so is not there.

For, like faith, prayer is not a matter of feeling or mood. Prayer may evoke strong emotions, but that is not prayer. Anyone who has practiced prayer for the least amount of time knows that the very *desire* for prayer is in itself a gift from God. It is not something we conjure up ourselves. Not that prayer is or should be drudgery, but a time will arise when one does not feel like praying. That time, however, is not a convenient excuse to refrain from prayer.

Prayer is not so much a "decision to pray" as it is a surrender to God. It is an emptying of the self. Prayer is letting go, the realization that we are not in control, but that God is. We do not even produce prayer, God does. We merely allow it to wash over us. In prayer the ego dies, and the true self cleaves to God. Because prayer is about surrender, because prayer is about denying the self, prayer is the antithesis of rugged individualism, to being in control, to the self-made woman or man. Prayer deepens in proportion to the degree to which we die to self and cleave to God. In prayer we discover that we stand before God naked and exposed. Thus, we see that we are totally dependent upon God. The account of Jesus' crucifixion in the Gospel of Mark is the example of the perfect prayer. Nailed to the cross, Jesus is mocked by criminals, Roman soldiers and by some of his fellow Jews. Jesus cries, "My God, My God, why have you forsaken me?" and there is no answer. Through all that, however, Jesus believes; he still clings to God in the darkest hour. Such is the model of perfect prayer. Such is the level of prayer for which we strive, that we still cling to God in the face of utter silence and darkness, for faith tells us that God is Emmanuel—"God is with us."

Silence is the sound of prayer. It is at the same time both the milieu of prayer and the mode of prayer. Silence calms our soul, quiets our thoughts. Not that we try to suppress our thoughts during prayer, for that would be impossible. Rather, while in prayer we do not allow our thoughts to distract us nor allow them to carry us away to a state of mind we do not want to be in. In prayer we strive to be still, to hear God, to rest in God.

For prayer is like sitting on the riverbank. We come to

the riverbank to watch the water drift by, allowing the lazy current of the river to lull us. Now and then a piece of driftwood slips by. We notice it, but we don't dwell upon it. What's important is the river, not the driftwood.

The deeper one descends into the silence and the longer one rests in God the more one realizes that words are superfluous to prayer. Prayer is not about words. Prayer is not about litanies. Prayer is about silence before the awesome God. "Silence, all mankind, in the presence of the LORD" (Zechariah 2:17); "But the LORD is in his holy temple; silence before him, all the earth!" (Habakkuk 2:20); "Be still and confess that I am God!" (Psalm 46:11); "Be still before the LORD; wait for God" (Psalm 37:7). This is not to say that prayer with words is inappropriate or useless. Obviously, such prayers are good. What it does mean, however, is that prayer—union with God—must go beyond the words. Words and litanies are merely the means by which we enter into silence, into the depths of our being, in order to rest in God. Prayer is not about concepts; it is about entering the mystery of God who is beyond all concepts. The anonymous author of *The Cloud of Unknowing* wrote in the fourteenth century:

> . . . it is equally useless to think you can nourish your contemplative work by considering God's attributes, his kindness or his dignity; or by thinking about Our Lady, the angels, or the saints; or about heaven, wonderful as these will be. It is far better to let your mind rest in the awareness of him in his naked existence and to love and praise him for what he is in himself. [1]

This resting silently and wordlessly in the presence of God has a name. It is called meditation. Meditation is practiced in a variety of ways, but the method described here— silently and wordlessly resting in God—is a very ancient form of Christian prayer. It is set steadfastly in the

Christian tradition. The history of Christian meditation stretches back beyond the fourteenth century of *The Cloud of Unknowing* to the Desert Fathers and Mothers of Egypt, Syria and Palestine of the fourth century. Evagrius Ponticus, Saint John Cassian and Saint Anthony the Great all practiced meditation. It has its roots in the Gospel story of Martha and Mary, in which Mary preferred sitting at the Master's feet to busying herself with the chores of hospitality.

In *The Chapters on Prayer*, Evagrius, born in A.D. 345 in what is now Turkey, wrote "Stand guard over your spirit, keeping it free of concepts at the time of prayer so that it may remain in its own calm"[2]; "Do not by any means strive to fashion some image or visualize some form at the time of prayer"[3]; "Happy is the spirit that attains to perfect formlessness at the time of prayer"[4]; "Happy is the spirit that attains to complete unconsciousness of all sensible experience at the time of prayer."[5] These sayings, composed sometime between 390 and 395, epitomize the monastic approach to prayer. They help the Christian to probe the depths of his or her "center" in order to discover and rest in God. Once at this center, the Christian is liberated from the self so that what remains is God. *Not* that we become God, but that God consumes our being, and we desire nothing but the love of God and to love God. In other words, we search into our center in order to transcend ourselves. All this is done in an atmosphere of silence and calm, where random thoughts and images are simply ignored, enabling one to rest in God. Saint John Cassian put it this way:

> This prayer centers on no contemplation of some image or other. It is masked by no attendant sounds or words. It is a fiery outbreak, an indescribable exaltation, and insatiable thrust of the soul. Free of what is sensed and seen, ineffable

in its groans and sighs, the soul pours itself out to God.[6]

Such forms of prayer sound odd or exotic to modern Christians who thrive on vocal or mental prayer, be it shouts of praise, heartfelt renditions of the Our Father or choruses of Hail Marys. It is not that meditation is better than any other form of prayer. It is not. But meditation is equally as good as any other form of prayer and just as accessible.

In an essay that appeared in the June 1998 issue of the *American Benedictine Review*, Cistercian monk Basil Pennington wrote that monasteries should be "places where persons can go to learn contemplative meditation just as Buddhist monasteries and centers are." He then continues, "How sad it would be if students could go through a Benedictine school and still think they had to go to the Buddhists to learn to meditate!"[7] How sad that children educated in any Christian school would believe only Buddhists meditate. If the exotic is what one seeks, one can do no better than to explore the ancient Christian wisdom of such people as John the Dwarf, Isaac of the Cells, Poemen the Shepherd or Paul the Simple.

Prayer is not about technique, however. Mediation is not some mathematical equation that, once you solve it, you automatically find God. Meditation is not a riddle to ponder, and having put all the pieces together, presto! You see God. Meditation is not method, but attitude; not a gadget, but a way of life.

This way of life is lived in humility. Humility is the knowledge that you have been created in another's image, God's image, and that your life is not your own. Dorotheos of Gaza, a sixth-century Syrian from Antioch, wrote that perfect humility is to attribute all virtuous actions to God.[8] Pride seeks to make God appear after pushing all the right buttons, after calculating the proper formulas, after saying the prescribed prayers over a predetermined span of time. Pride wants God to conform to you. Humility is surrender to God. Humility understands that one's virtue springs not from within the self, but forth from God. Humility seeks union with God in a life lived in tranquility and love; in a life that transcends the self and reaches for God. The proud demand God's appearance; the humble cry for God's embrace.

In the end, then, prayer is not something you "do," nor is meditation something distinct from prayer. Prayer becomes the way you live your life. Prayer and your life become one and the same. Meditation and life meld into the arms of God, and the self disappears. All that remains is God.

NOTES

1 *The Cloud of Unknowing*, trans. William Johnston (New York: Doubleday, 1973), p. 54.

2 *Praktikos & Chapters on Prayer*, trans. John Eudes Bamberger (Kalamazoo, Mich.: Cistercian Publications, 1972), p. 66.

3 *Ibid.*, p. 74.

4 *Ibid.*, p. 75.

5 *Ibid.*, p. 75.

6 Saint John Cassian, *Conferences*, p. 138.

7 Basil Pennington, "The Benedictine Contribution to Evangelization," *American Benedictine Review* 49 (1998), p. 228.

8 Dorotheos of Gaza, *Discourses & Sayings* (Kalamazoo, Mich.: Cistercian Publications, 1977), p. 98.

12

More Prayer

Scripture is the passage to prayer. In the days before the printing press, when the Bible had to be copied by hand, copies of the Bible were few. Most folks did not have an easily accessible Bible to read or to consult. Furthermore, many people in the times prior to the printing press were illiterate. So, even if one had access to a copy of the Bible, such access did not guarantee the Bible could be read. Consequently, people of this time tended to memorize large chunks of the Bible. Either through reading passages themselves, or having passages from the Bible read to them, people mulled over and over passages of Scripture until they learned these passages by heart.

Memorization and knowing by heart are not synonymous. I have memorized telephone numbers, my social security number and e-mail addresses. I use these numbers everyday, and when I use them I do not have to make an effort to bring them to mind. The numbers or the addresses are purely functional: I punch in the telephone number and, seconds later, I'm talking to someone. The number I used to access the person is meaningless as soon as the person with whom I wish to speak comes on the line.

As a child I had to memorize Longfellow's "The Village Blacksmith." I can still recall portions of the poem. Now and then—once a year, perhaps—I will run through Longfellow's famous poem just to see how much I have retained. Though portions of the poem are still with me, the words mean nothing to me. They are just words.

Some of the psalms I know by heart. These words are not just stored in my head; they live in my heart. When I bring them to mind, the words are not merely recited as if they were Longfellow's poem, they are chewed and gnawed upon so that I can digest them. They are internalized and mulled over. The words of the psalm become part of my being. They create a passage, allowing me access to God. This passage, then, draws me closer to God. The words are prayer.

Monasticism has a special tradition with Scripture. That tradition is known as *lectio divina,* or holy reading. First and foremost, *lectio* is prayer. In *lectio* you do not so much read Scripture as hear it with your heart. *Lectio* is not an academic exercise. In *lectio* you do not read the Scriptures to decipher theology or prove a point. *Lectio* is not about knowing God, it is about experiencing God. *Lectio* is about listening.

Lectio is not a devotional. In a devotional, the person is active, petitioning, praising or beseeching God. The line of action goes from person to God. *Lectio* is just the opposite; God comes to the person and the person listens.

Lectio divina begins with a deep reverence for the Word. In Bible study, one may mark in the text, underlining certain passages or scribbling comments in the margins of the page. That is not the case in *lectio.* Here, you do not impose your opinions or thoughts on the text.

You do not, however, simply grab a copy of the Bible,

flop down in a chair, open the book and begin immediately to plow through Paul. Before entering into *lectio*, you cut yourself off from where you have been: going to another room in the house, leaving the house and going to church, stepping outside in the quiet of the yard or a park. Having found the appropriate site for prayer, you prepare your mind and soul for prayer. You take some deep breaths; you ask for God's presence. One such prayer might be, "Come, Holy Spirit, fill the hearts of your faithful, and enkindle in them the fire of your love." Many kneel or light candles as this prayer is prayed. The idea is that you are separating yourself—emotionally, physically and spiritually—from what you had been doing prior to coming to *lectio*.

You begin by reading the text *slowly*, aloud if desired. Reading aloud dispels distractions and helps to internalize the words being read. There is something about words rolling off the tongue that gives them more impact. You read until a certain word or phrase strikes a chord. That word or phrase is then repeated over and over, allowing it to seep into the soul. This rumination *is the prayer*. This is the essence of *lectio*. The chewing and gnawing of the Word brings God into the depths of your being.

How much text is to be covered in one sitting? That is the beauty of *lectio*. There are no rules, and therefore no pressure, about the amount of text to be read at any one sitting. One time, only a single verse may be covered. At another time, a half of a verse may be read. Still other times, several verses of Scripture may be covered. Several months may be required to read an entire book of the Bible. The amount of text covered is never the issue. The issue is allowing what is read to be mulled over in the heart, allowing God to enter your being.

Although the amount of text to be covered is never important, consistently practicing *lectio* is important. *Lectio* should become a habit. Breaking open the Word should be a regular form of prayer.

We bring no preconceived notions or agendas to this form of prayer. In *lectio* we allow God into our hearts. The idea is to allow God to act upon us, not we to act upon God. In *lectio* we accept what comes. Love of Scripture and use of it as prayer anchor us in the Word. In praying the Scriptures, *lectio*, we emulate the Master who prayed the Scriptures, prayed them even when he was dying on the cross.

The Christian does not pray alone, however. The Christian belongs to the Body of Christ, who is the People of God, which is the church. The Christian may experience prayer individually, but the prayer is shared by the entire Body. *Lectio* may be prayed alone in the quiet of a room, but the prayer of *lectio* transcends the individual and is presented to God by the entire Body through Jesus. The foot of the body does not walk independently of the leg or the mind. The one who prays *lectio* does not pray alone, either, but is joined by the entire Body.

The Body in prayer expands the presence of God in the world. God already fills the universe, but the Body in prayer makes God palpable. This is the majesty of the Incarnation: that God shows us that he is with us. Prayer is nothing more than the repetition of the Incarnation, for prayer is the reminder that God is with us—Emmanuel.

Hence, Christians are an incarnational people. For the Christian, God is not some remote being who is "out there" in the sky, who dwells in a different dimension. For the Christian, God is on this earth; God's image is in other people. *Not* that people are God, but that humanity possesses the spark of divinity due to the implantation of God's image in it. The man Jesus, when he walked this earth, was that spark exploded into a fire. Jesus, our brother in the flesh, showed us what that spark looks like when totally dedicated to God. Jesus illustrated the nobility of humanity.

Humanity is noble because it has the ability to communicate with God. To be fully human, then, we must pray. William of Saint-Thierry wrote, "Prayer is the affection of a man who clings to God."[1] Jesus is the one through whom we pray, for Jesus is the face of God, the face who walked this earth. Scripture is the passageway to God. Through Scripture we look into the depths of our being, discover that spark of the image, then explode beyond ourselves to love God and neighbor, and to love as Jesus loves us.

Prayer is the fire of God in the hearts and on the lips of humanity. That fire derives from the spark of the image imbedded within humanity, and it is the image that is humanity's glory. "The man of God is found worthy to become not God but what God is, that is to say man becomes through grace what God is by nature."[2]

That would be: holy.

NOTES

[1] William of Saint-Thierry, *Golden Epistle*, p. 71.

[2] *Ibid.*, p. 96.

13

The Little Hours

A rule of thumb I set for myself when I am at the Monastic Center is that I head for choir fifteen minutes before Office is to begin. Of course, circumstances may dictate otherwise—work, meetings and so on—but I am almost always making my way to choir fifteen minutes before Office.

Why? For no big theological reason, really, but just to sit in the church alone and "warm up," as it were, for prayer. Saint John Cassian wrote in his *Conferences*:

> Before the time of prayer we must put ourselves in the state of mind we would wish to have in us when we actually pray. It is an inexorable fact that the condition of the soul at the time of prayer depends upon what shaped it beforehand. The soul will rise to the heights of heaven or plunge into the things of earth, depending upon where it lingered before the time of prayer. [1]

I enjoy being in the church during the Little Hours because the sunlight streams through the windows, flooding the church with light and warmth. During Lauds and the long night Office only darkness is outside the windows. But for these Little Hours the church is bathed in light, and the church takes on a whole new feel, a whole new demeanor. Through Lauds, and especially all through the night Office, the church seems stern and cold. Even if the night Office holds that special feeling of mystery and awe, the sense of austerity of the night never seems to leave you. Not so the Little Hours. At those hours the church seems almost playful. The dancing light, the sounds of awakened nature outside the windows give the Little Hours a sense of joy, even giddiness.

So what are these Little Hours? They are the hours of prayer called Terce, Sext and None; the third (terce), sixth (sext) and ninth (none) hours of prayer. The third, sixth and ninth hours as reckoned from when? From 6:00 A.M. Hence, Terce is prayed around nine o'clock in the morning, Sext around noon and None, some nine hours from 6:00 A.M. at around three o'clock in the afternoon, although this time may differ somewhat from monastery to monastery, depending on their work schedule. The reckoning from 6:00 A.M. is a holdover from the ancient Roman reckoning of time.

These hours of prayer are referred to as "little" for a couple of reasons. First, though important, they do not rank in importance with Lauds and Vespers, "the two hinges on which the daily office turns."[2] Second, Terce, Sext and None are not as long in duration as are the other hours. The Little Hours are brief, usually about ten minutes in length. Hence, they are "little." Yet praying the Little Hours helps monks fulfill the psalmist's adage, "Seven times a day I praise you because your edicts are just" (Psalm 119:164).

The psalms that make up the Little Hours are from the gradual psalms. The gradual psalms are numbers 119 through 133, and are also called "songs of ascent," because they were sung by the pilgrims as they were going *up* to

Jerusalem. These psalms are comparatively short and easy to memorize, thereby making them popular with pilgrims making their way to the Temple.

At New Melleray at Terce, Psalms 119 through 121 are chanted Monday through Saturday. At Sext, Psalms 122 through 124 are sung on Mondays, Wednesdays and Fridays. On Tuesdays, Thursdays and Saturdays Psalms 128 through 130 are sung. For None, Psalms 125 through 127 are chanted on Mondays, Wednesdays and Fridays, while on Tuesdays and Thursdays, Psalms 131 through 132 are used. The longest psalm in the psalter, number 118, is spread out over two Sundays, requiring the three Little Hours both days to complete the one long psalm. (See Appendix 2 on pages 120 and 121.)

But before you go looking up these psalms in your Bible, remember that New Melleray, like many Cistercian monasteries, uses the Greek Septuagint numeration of the psalms, not the Hebrew numeration. What this means is that for most of the psalms the Septuagint numeration is one behind the Hebrew. So in the above account of the Little Hours at New Melleray, for example, the Terce psalms for Monday through Friday are Psalms 120 through 122 in the Hebrew numeration. Below is a comparative table of the two systems.

Greek Septuagint	Hebrew
1–8	1–8
9	9–10
10–112	11–113
113	114–115
114–115	116
116–145	117–146
146–147	147
148–150	148–150

NOTES

[1] Saint John Cassian, *Conferences*, pp. 139-40.

[2] *Vatican Council II: The Conciliar and Post Conciliar Documents*, p. 25.

14

Work

After the final blessing is given at the conclusion of None, I glance at my watch: 1:55. I quickly leave the church and bound up the stairs to my cell. I slip off my smock, don a sweatshirt and a hat, then hurry back down the stairs. Brother Placid will be out front in his pickup truck at two o'clock sharp and I must be there waiting for him.

It is time for work. The associates in the Monastic Center are expected to work in the afternoons from after None to around 4:30. Work is also available to the associates in the morning from after Terce until 11:00, but that work period is optional. During this time of year, the October harvest, work usually takes the associates out to the garden and pumpkin patch. Assignment of work comes in the morning at breakfast. The associates eat together in a small room just off the dining room, and Brother Placid will stop by to assign work while they are eating. "The garden today, fellas," he might say. Or, pointing a finger at one of us, he might say, "You go to the kitchen." On this particular morning the garden was assigned to me, and I was happy, for the weather was beautiful.

Brother Placid pulled up in front of the house at two o'clock. The beat-up blue Ford pickup he was driving had seen better days: rusty, the inside dirty, the seats ripped, the dashboard littered with paper. The bed of the truck was strewn with empty buckets, battered pairs of gloves and tiny bits of gravel. Brother William slid into the seat next to Brother Placid, while St. Louis Paul, Matt and I hopped into the bed of the truck and settled there.

The truck drove through the gate bearing the sign, "Monastic Enclosure: Do not enter," and headed for the back of the house. Here was the garden and farm. In the distance, although I could not see it, I heard the whir of a combine. Brother Placid drove us to the tool shed. Here, we picked up some extra pairs of gloves and other tools.

"Paul, you and Bill wash potatoes," Brother Placid instructed. Buckets of potatoes stood behind the tool shed. Also there was a garden hose. One dumped the produce onto one or both of the mesh tables that stood behind the tool shed and, using the hose, washed the produce that had recently been picked from the garden.

Pointing his gnarled finger at Matt and me, Brother Placid continued, "You two come with me." Matt and I jumped back into the bed of the truck and Brother Placid gunned the truck back to life.

We drove back to the garden. "Pick beans," Placid said, "these rows here." He pointed to the two long rows of green beans. Matt and I pulled several buckets from the truck bed, then Brother Placid drove off, the truck sputtering.

Matt started at the end of one row, while I walked in the opposite direction and began on the end of another row. I sat down in the dirt, slipped on my gloves and began picking beans.

The sun was warm. The air was still. Only the rumbling of the distant combine broke the quiet. Above me the sky was a deep blue without a trace of clouds. Matt and I picked beans in silence.

Again my mind was swamped with thoughts of how foolish all this was. Is this any way to spend your vacation, I asked myself, sitting in the dirt picking beans? But I was neither disturbed nor anxious. Yes, this was the way I wanted to spend some of my vacation. What others might think of it did not matter to me. How liberating was that frame of mind!

When I first came to the Monastic Center, and when I first worked out in the fields, I prayed psalms and other prayers silently to myself. I was trying to make holy what I was *doing*. But it soon dawned on me that what I was *doing* was holy precisely because I was doing it for God. The work did not need my prayers; the work itself was the prayer.

But how often do I feel that way about my own work at the library back in Indiana? How often do I view the phone calls and the urgent requests from the physicians as prayer? In truth, not very often at all. It is easy to see beauty and prayer and God in the work that you perform only for several days out of the year. It is more difficult to see beauty and prayer in the work you perform day in and day out, year after year. That, of course, is the lot of these men who live and work at New Melleray all their lives. Working in the kitchen, the fields, the laundry and the workshops of New Melleray Abbey is their job, their prayer. It is not a retreat or a pilgrimage as it is for the associates. The community of New Melleray must daily make the familiar prayerful and the mundane holy.

That is the challenge for those living outside the monastery as well. Work *can* be prayerful, the ordinary *can* be holy if all is performed for love of God. Rafael Baron was an oblate brother in a Cistercian monastery in Spain in the 1930s. Baron wrote in his journal:

> Loving God in the world through words is as valid as doing
> so in a Trappist monastery in silence. The thing is to do
> something for him . . . to be mindful of him; the place, the
> situation, the occupation are unimportant. God can make
> me as holy by peeling potatoes as by ruling an empire. [1]

Nothing is accomplished if you come to New Melleray, work in the fields, wax poetic about it and then return to your place of employment whining and complaining about the work. All that will have been accomplished is to have made the Monastic Center experience a romantic and sentimental aside.

After an hour or so, my back began to hurt. I tried kneeling as Matt was doing, but that only exacerbated the pain.

I sat back down. Now and then a truck loaded with monks would pass by on the dirt road and we would wave at one another. Then all would be quiet once more.

My bucket was nearly full with green beans. The only beans I was leaving on the vines were the puny ones, as Brother Placid instructed. I was just beginning to start a new bucket when Brother Placid drove up in his truck.

"Let's go to the pumpkin patch," he said leaning out the window. So Matt and I put our buckets of beans in the truck bed, hopped on the tailgate and Brother Placid took off, Matt's and my legs dangling over the gate of the truck.

But we didn't go directly to the pumpkins. Instead, we stopped by the corn rows and picked corn. Brother Placid showed us how to pluck the ear from the stalk, peel back the husk and leave the husk attached to the ear at the stem. Matt and I walked through the tall stalks picking corn for about half an hour.

When we had filled five buckets, Brother Placid told us to load it all up into the truck. We did so and then we headed to the pumpkin patch.

The pumpkin patch was back in the far corner of the farm and down at the bottom of a small hill. As we gained the crest of the hill in Brother Placid's truck, the combine I had intermittently heard finally came into view. It was harvesting the large cornfield to the east of us.

Brother Placid handed me a long-handled cutter. I was to cut the pumpkin from the vine, leaving about four inches of stem on the pumpkin, then roll the gourd over in order to expose the dirt spot. Matt and Brother Placid would then brush off the dirt spot and load the pumpkins into the bed of the truck. That long-handled tool cut through the thick coarse vine like butter, requiring no real pressure on my part.

A little over a dozen pumpkins were loaded into the truck before Brother Placid decided that was enough. Now we had buckets of green beans and corn, plus a dozen or so pumpkins, in the bed of the truck. Matt and I hopped back onto the tailgate and Brother Placid drove back to the tool shed where the washing station was located.

"Might have gone over to pick walnuts," Brother Placid commented, when Matt and I noted that neither Brother William nor St. Louis Paul was around.

Matt, Brother Placid and I unloaded the beans and the pumpkins, but Placid told us to leave the corn on the truck. Matt and I began washing the beans and, without comment, Brother Placid got back into his truck and drove off. Though the temperature was in the upper 50s to low 60s, the water was very cold, and our hands soon were cold and red.

As we finished washing the final two pumpkins, Brother Placid returned in his truck with Brother William and St. Louis Paul. All of us then reloaded the produce onto the truck, including the potatoes that Brother William and St. Louis Paul had washed earlier.

"Let's see how much of this we can sell," said Brother Placid after the produce was loaded. I assumed we were headed out front to where all the produce was sold, but no, we stopped at the walnut trees in order to pick up walnuts from the ground.

"I guess we didn't get enough," said St. Louis Paul to Brother William. By this time all the buckets on the truck were full of produce. Since all of us were wearing sweat-shirts, we simply used the bottom portion of our sweatshirts as pouches to hold the walnuts. We were not there five minutes, however, when Brother Placid told us to load up the truck with what we had. We did so, and then Placid drove us to the front of the house.

The corn, pumpkins and walnuts we unloaded and placed on the ground at the edge of the parking lot. Nailed to a nearby tree was a cardboard sign listing the prices of the produce in ink from a red marker: "Small pumpkins— $1.00, Large pumpkins—$2.50." Next to the tree was an empty coffee can in which to place your money. The buyer was the judge of what was a large pumpkin and what was a small one.

After unloading the corn, pumpkins and walnuts, Brother Placid drove around to the east side of the house where the kitchen was located. "Refrigerator 3 for the beans and potatoes, men," said Brother Placid, "and that'll be it for the day." The four of us grabbed the buckets of green beans and potatoes and headed for the kitchen. We placed all the buckets in the walk-in refrigerator.

I would have no problem getting to sleep tonight.

NOTE

[1] Rafael Baron, "Life and Writings of Brother M. Rafael Baron (III)," *Cistercian Studies Quarterly* 35 (2000), p. 86.

15

The Cell

A monk's room is called a cell. The word "cell" is not to imply a prison cell; the monk may enter and exit the cell at will. Rather, the monk's cell is a place of refuge.

The importance of the cell to monasticism is difficult to overemphasize. Indeed, the cell may be the oldest component of monasticism. The Desert Fathers and Mothers, those hermits and monks who inhabited the deserts of Egypt in the fourth, fifth and sixth centuries, spoke of the cell frequently and emphatically:

> A brother came to Scetis to visit Abba Moses and asked for a word. The old man said to him, "Go, sit in your cell, and your cell will teach you everything."[1]
>
> He [Anthony the Great] also said, "Just as fish die if they stay too long out of water, so the monks who loiter outside their cells or pass their time with men of the world lose the intensity of inner peace. So like a fish going towards the sea, we must hurry to reach our cell, for fear that if we delay outside we will lose our interior watchfulness."[2]

In more recent times, Thomas Merton has written: "The cell is the place where man comes to know himself first of all that he may know God."[3]

I am writing this in my cell in the Monastic Center. I have come here to be alone. I have come here to be ensconced in silence. I have come here to help myself seek and experience God, to fulfill the adage of the Desert Fathers, "sit in your cell, and your cell will teach you everything." Today it is my cell.

But is this really my cell? I am in this room only on retreat, and sometimes not even then, for I have been assigned other rooms in the Monastic Center as well. When I leave New Melleray, someone else will occupy "my cell." How, then, can it be my cell?

It is my cell, for I have chosen it to be so. I was assigned this room, but I have chosen to be at New Melleray. When I return home, my cell may be a bedroom or even the bathroom. My cell might be a nearby chapel that has Eucharistic Adoration. My cell may be the parish where I attend noon Mass during the work week. My cell may be a combination of all these places over the period of a single day. The cell is anyplace where the lay monastic can be alone and in silence with God. The cell is portable.

The cell is where the lay monastic encounters the awesomeness of God. Alone in the cell, the monk has no recourse but prayer, no place to hide except in God. Here, the false self falls to the floor with a thud. The silence and solitude of the cell allow for no pretense, only the humble realization that one is totally dependent on God. The cell will either crush you or ennoble you, frighten you or cheer you. You either want to enter it or you want to flee it. As Our Lord bemoaned those indifferent toward him, so the cell spews forth the halfhearted; it does not tolerate apathy.

If the oratory is the heart of the monastery, the cell is the soul. For from the cell flows the essence of monasticism—union with God. William of Saint-Thierry wrote,

"The cell is holy ground and a holy place in which the Lord and his servant often talk together as a man does with his friend."[4] It is from the cell that Office, work and prayer convey meaning for the lay monastic. The cell extends and prolongs the Office; it deepens the prayer and dignifies the work. The cell is where the lay monastic listens to the mysterious silence of God and, in imitation of Our Lady, ponders it. Everything else in the monastic life emanates from the silent solitude of the cell. The cell is the monastery in miniature.

The cell is also a place of battle. Here the monk fights the demons of acedia, or apathy, and self-will. Acedia is the opponent of peace. Acedia whispers into the ear of the monk that everything she is trying to do is useless. Acedia frequently reminds the monk how long the day is dragging on, and aren't you bored with it all? Acedia likes to show the monk the long empty years that lie before him in this life of endless repetition of work and prayer, work and prayer, and you really think you will be able to endure that mind-numbing monotony? In essence, acedia urges the monk to surrender her charism, because it is too difficult, too trivial and too boring, not worth the effort. Acedia likes to remind the monk that the church has more important things for him to be doing—feeding the poor, visiting prisoners, fighting social injustice. Alone in her cell, the monk is vulnerable to these attacks. Ironically, however, the cell is the ideal battleground to thwart acedia, for the cell is a holy place (remember William of Saint-Thierry), and the cell reminds the monk that the whole purpose of his life is to rely on God, and that God is bigger than any bout of acedia.

The demon of self-will is no less vicious, merely more subtle. Self-will is the opponent of humility. Self-will is the monk's image of herself. The monk sees himself in a certain

light. A monk *does this* or a monk *does that*. A monk is supposed to think in *this* fashion, say *these* things. This is not a
question of the monk *flattering* herself, rather it is a preconceived notion of the charism that does not conform to reality. More importantly, however, self-will smothers the true
image resting within the monk: the image of God. One of
the functions of the cell, then, is to force the monk to confront self-will and overcome it.

The first word in Benedict's Rule is *listen*. This is the
primary function of the cell, to provide a place for the
monk to listen to God. Sometimes the silence is euphoric.
Other times the silence of the cell is frightening or puzzling
or downright boring. At these times it seems as though God
has withdrawn and completely disappeared. Merton provides a good course of action when this occurs.

> . . . the work of the cell . . . is done in silence and not
> according to one's own choice or the pressure of necessity,
> but in obedience to God. But the voice of God is not heard
> at every moment, and part of the "work of the cell" is atten-
> tion so that one may not miss any sound of that Voice. [5]

The danger for the lay monastic is that removing himself
from the cell during these dry times is so easy. She can
merely walk out of the bedroom or come up from the basement and walk back into "family life." But it is precisely
during these dry times that it is important for the lay
monastic to stay put in the cell. For if the lay monastic can
remain calm, he will overcome this bout of acedia and
emerge cleaving all the more to God. Above all, the lay
monastic must remember the reason she entered the cell in
the first place: to be delivered from her own "ego-image"
and seek union with God. [6] The function of the cell is to
provide the opportunity to do just that.

Jesus frequently retreated to the mountains to pray.

The cell is the monastic's mountain, a retreat where he can pray. Prayer is the function of the cell.

NOTES

[1] *Sayings of the Desert Fathers*, trans. Benedicta Ward (Kalamazoo, Mich.: Cistercian Publications, 1975), p. 139.

[2] *Ibid.*, p. 3.

[3] Thomas Merton, *Contemplation in a World of Action*, p. 268.

[4] William of Saint-Thierry, *Golden Epistle*, p. 22.

[5] Thomas Merton, *Journals of Thomas Merton*, vol. 5 (New York: HarperSanFrancisco, 1997), pp. 254-5.

[6] Thomas Merton, *Contemplation in a World of Action*, p. 298.

16

Rebel

In the movie, *The Wild One*, Marlon Brando portrays a motorcycle tough named Johnny. Johnny and his gang of bikers blow into a small town one day and proceed to bluster and to bully and belittle the locals.

Early on in the movie, there is a scene in which Johnny and his pals are dancing with some local girls. One of these girls notices the initials B.R.M.C. etched on the back of the black leather jackets worn by Johnny and his bikers and asks her biker dancing partner what the initials stand for. "Black Rebels Motorcycle Club," comes the response. By this time the couple has danced over near Johnny, who is leaning against the jukebox watching the dancing and enjoying the music. The girl then asks Johnny, "Hey Johnny, what are you rebelling against?" Johnny replies, "Whadda'ya got?"

The rebel has long been with us. He is often admired and frequently romanticized. Even the American icon is a rebel—the Cowboy. The Cowboy thumbs his nose at the constrictions of the civilized East and heads for the wide-open spaces of the West. The Cowboy adheres to a "code" of integrity and justice. But most of all, the Cowboy prizes individualism and pragmatism. He simply wishes to be left alone to do his job as he sees fit, without interference from "outsiders," whether from government, church or community.

Johnny and the Cowboy are rebels in the culture of self. The image they seek to elevate is their own.

The Christian, too, must be a rebel, but not in the vein of Johnny or the Cowboy. The Christian must be a rebel against the culture of self. The Book of Wisdom says, "For God formed man to be imperishable; the *image of his own nature he made him*" (Wisdom 2:23; emphasis added). The rebellion of the Christian, then, consists in seeking daily to uncover the image of God that resides within. The Book of Ezekiel says, "I will give you a new heart and place a new spirit within you, taking from your bodies your stony hearts and giving you *natural hearts*. I will put *my spirit* within you . . ." (Ezekiel 36:26–7; emphasis added). The beauty of Christianity is that not only is God Emmanuel, God *with* us, God is also *in* humanity through Jesus. The Incarnation, then, is the personification of creation, the apogee of all creation, showing humanity what that spark of divinity that is within us, that "spirit" Ezekiel speaks of, looks like and acts like—Jesus of Nazareth, the Christ.

But not only that, the Incarnation makes us more like God. William of Saint-Thierry wrote:

> Christ the Bridegroom offered to his Bride the Church, so to speak, a kiss from heaven, when the Word made flesh drew so near to her that he wedded her to himself; and so wedded her that he united her to himself, in order that God might become man, and man might become God. [1]

Human beings, however, seek to polish the images of themselves, ignoring the image of the divine that is within each of them. The divine image subsequently atrophies and is tarnished, which is what we call sin. Aelred of Rievaulx, a twelfth-century Cistercian abbot, put it this way:

> By abusing free choice, then, he diverted his love from that changeless good and, blinded by his own self-centeredness, he directed his love to what was inferior. Thus without drawing from the true good and deviating toward what of itself was not good, where he anticipated gain he found loss, and by perversely loving himself he lost both himself and God. Thus it very justly came about that someone who sought the likeness of God in defiance of God, the more he wanted to become similar to God out of curiosity, the more dissimilar he became through self-centeredness. Therefore, the image of God became disfigured in man without becoming wholly destroyed. [2]

True rebellion, then, consists in restoring the image of God, the image God breathed into humanity and which humanity tarnished. It is a battle against the false self in an effort to recapture the true self. In order to find one's true self, one must know oneself. William of Saint-Thierry writes:

> Be wholly present to yourself, therefore, and employ yourself wholly in knowing yourself and knowing whose image you are, and likewise in discerning and understanding what you are and what you can do in him whose image you are. [3]

This is a lifelong and never-ending rebellion, one sparked not by the will of the person, but by the gift of God.

This rebellion takes the form of love. That which makes the Christian a rebel, then, is the decision to love. This choice to love can only be sparked within the person by God, for humanity is unable to muster this desire independently of God. This spark of love we call grace. The Christian answers the call to love, because the Master instructed his followers to do so. Love is the essence of the gospel of Jesus of Nazareth, who commanded his followers to love one another as he loved them (John 15:12), and who flatly exclaimed that eternal life was gained by loving God and neighbor (Luke 10:25–28).

To choose to love means to deny the self, for love is selfless. Love seeks the good of the other before that of the self. Again, this love cannot be had but by the help of God, *not* because it is contrary to human nature (remember Ezekiel), but because it is contrary to human *inclination*. It is *natural* to love God; it is unnatural to do otherwise. Because of the Fall, however, human beings are inclined to love themselves first. Sin, then, is the corruption of love, the confusion of objects of love, the deception of the self to think only of the self. Sin is the ultimate deception, for it persuades human beings to love themselves above all things. Jesus, the rebel par excellence, insisted on the complete reversal of this outlook. He died showing humanity how far one might have to go in pursuit of love of God and neighbor.

As society grows ever more secular, this rebellion of love will grow ever more visible, not because it will be heralded, but because it will be scorned. It will be seen as aberrant. Christendom is behind us, buried. Those practicing the rebellion will soon be viewed as quaint, as odd. In 1961 Merton wrote:

> We are living in a world that used to be Christian—and Hindu, Moslem, Buddhist. In the west we are in the post-Christian age—and all over the world it will soon be the same. The religions will be for the minority. The world as a whole is going to be not pagan but irreligious. Hence we are already living, and will live more and more, in a world that we cannot look upon precisely as "ours" in any external and obvious sense. . . . We will certainly survive, but as genuine aliens and exiles. And perhaps this is as it should be. Yet we should not for all that become inert and inactive. But our activity must take into account this new dimension

of a humility that has at last come to check our illusion of a politically successful Christendom. This sounds like defeatism and I am ready to revise and qualify it. But I confess it looks to me like sober truth. It does not make one less a Christian. On the contrary, it confirms me in my dependence on the Gospel message and in my dedication to Christ![4]

The monk is a component in this rebellion of love, this dedication to Christ. In truth, the monk has been in the vanguard of the rebellion ever since men and women fled to the deserts of Egypt and Palestine in the fourth century. As the Cowboy expressed a form of rebellion in his time, and as Johnny expressed another kind of rebellion more recently, so the monk has rebelled quietly throughout the centuries. The silent life stood as antidote even at the height of Christendom. Now, however, the monk in the cloister is joined with the monk in the world, and their rebellion will only grow more pronounced, more visible.

For the nature of the monk is at odds with the prevailing culture. Nothing in our culture is more useless than monks. The diocesan clergy, at least, provide a service for people. Lay ministers do likewise. But monks? What task do they perform? What service do they provide? Who do they help? What do they *do*?

Which is exactly the point. The monk is the antithesis of everything the prevailing culture esteems. The monk is poor, powerless and prayerful. The monk retires to a cell and prays. The monk is therefore useless to a culture that measures worth by wealth, power, status and, most of all, utility. Not only does the monk lack these attributes, the monk actively refutes them. This only adds to the rebelliousness of the monk.

Because the monk "does nothing," he is un-American. Love of country is not at issue here. America was founded upon liberty, but America thrives on utilitarianism. America acts. The monk sits. America is bold. The monk seeks humility. America is the rugged individualist—the Cowboy—beholden to no one. The monk lives in a community and answers to an abbot and to God. America is ever on the move, impatient with being in one place. The monk vows stability.

The monk is un-American in another way. At the dawn of the twenty-first century, there is a strong tendency in America to confuse freedom with license, uninhibited action. There is a reluctance among Americans to tolerate restraints on behavior and a strain of intolerance for those who advocate such restraints. The monk, on the other hand, seeks to die to all those desires of the heart that enslave us to selfish actions. By doing so, the monk attains *freedom*. But this true freedom many Americans view as inhibition, as a stifling of the "true inner self," as an infringement upon constitutionally protected rights. Jean Leclercq, the twentieth-century Benedictine, wrote:

> The fundamental attitude of the soul united to God is detachment from itself. When a soul lives habitually in this state of radical renouncement, then at times it is given a realization of its own nothingness. [5]

Which brings us back to Johnny, the motorcycle rebel. The answer to Johnny's question—"Whadda'ya got?"—is simple. The answer is . . . nothing. Nothing can be offered Johnny that he will not "rebel" against. Johnny believes himself to be a rebel; in fact, he is a conservative. Johnny conserves and perpetuates the myth that he is going against the grain of society by behaving in an antisocial fashion. In reality, Johnny merely builds upon and extends the trajectory of the selfishness that is already around him. He does so, however, in a flamboyant manner, giving him and others around him the illusion that he is doing something different, that he is "rebelling." Furthermore, since Johnny sees everything surrounding him as only an extension of his own desires and cravings, there is *nothing* out there to rebel against, only himself. Johnny is not rebelling; he is perpetuating the self. The joke is that Johnny cannot see this; he believes in his own "rebellion."

The irony is that "nothingness," in the sense that Leclercq uses it, is precisely the answer to Johnny's searching. But Johnny is unable to see that. He and his buddies travel from place to place looking for what is "real," but "reality" always seems to elude them. Johnny and his buddies are desperate, then, grasping at straws, "rebelling" against anything and everything. Hence, his answer to the young lady's question makes perfect sense to him. What am I rebelling against? Well, what have you got?

Our culture views rebellion as Johnny does. It should come as no surprise, then, that the culture looks askance at the monk. True rebellion has nothing to do with politics or economics or flouting prevailing mores with modes of dress and adornment. The true rebel? The person who seeks detachment from the self by recapturing the image of God that resides within. The monk knows this, and with the help of God's grace, rebels. The monk, though, is not working without a frame of reference. Before the monk and within the monk is the ultimate rebel—Jesus of Nazareth. As Paul says, "All of us . . . are being transformed into the same image . . . as from the Lord who is the Spirit" (2 Corinthians 3:18).

NOTES

[1] William of Saint-Thierry, *Exposition on the Song of Songs*, p. 25.

[2] Aelred of Rievaulx, *Mirror of Charity* (Kalamazoo, Mich.: Cistercian Publications, 1990), p. 93.

[3] William of Saint-Thierry, *Exposition on the Song of Songs*, p. 53.

[4] Thomas Merton, *Journals of Thomas Merton*, vol. 4, p. 138.

[5] Jean Leclercq, *Alone with God* (New York: Farrar, Straus, Cudahy, 1961), p. 162.

17

Compline

The day is behind us now. Work is over, we have eaten our final meal of the day, our meditation is done and our *lectio* is on hold for tomorrow. Sleep awaits us. But one more trip to the church is on tap, another communal activity is yet to be made, one last prayer is to be sung: Compline.

At this time of the year, October, darkness has fallen by the time Compline commences at 7:30 in the evening. So, as I enter the church, darkness greets me just as it did sixteen hours earlier at Vigils. When I slip into my choir stall I have no need to fuss with the books, for the lights will never be turned up for me to read them anyway. This is a prayer from the heart, sung totally from memory, in the dark.

The psalms? Psalms 4 and 90 (91). Always. Never varies. Count on it. The psalms are sung not to the accompaniment of the organ, but to the guitar. A small group of the brothers slip out of choir and stand in the space between the choir stalls. They face the altar; those in choir face the four brothers. The brother standing who holds the guitar lightly strums a chord, and we are off.

When I call, answer me, O God of justice;

From anguish you released me, have mercy and
hear me.

This is a lullaby for grown men. The rolling rhythm of the
simple melody, the familiar words and the darkness, in
essence, lull the men to sleep. Compline is a prayer begging
protection "from the terror of the night," with the psalmist
assuring the men that "under [God's] wings you will find
refuge."

Like its counterparts, Lauds and Vespers, Compline has
a canticle proper to it—the Nunc Dimittis, or the Canticle
of Simeon. The Responsory preceding the Nunc Dimittis
echoes the theme of the Compline psalms—protection:

Into your hands, O Lord, I commend my Spirit.
It is you who will redeem me, O Lord my God.
I commend my Spirit.

After the presider begs God for a "restful night and a peaceful death," the Hour ends with a spotlight rising above the
image of the Virgin that stands near the altar. The monks
turn to face the image and sing a cappella the "Salve
Regina" to the Blessed Mother.

At the completion of the Marian hymn, the brothers
step out of their stalls and walk in two rows toward the
abbot. The brothers bow as they approach the abbot, and
the abbot blesses them with holy water. With that, the
Great Silence begins. The brothers climb the stairs back to
their individual cells for their night's sleep. It is not quite
8:00 P.M.

Tomorrow morning we will start all over again.

18

Michigan City

*F*our months have passed since I have returned from New Melleray. About a foot of snow is on the ground here, on this second day of February. The snow is a remnant of a lake-effect storm that blew through a week ago. Beautiful to behold and fun to play in, it nevertheless closed schools and the outlet mall. You know it is a bad snowstorm when the mall closes. Now the snow is dirty and full of pebbles and a nuisance. With the temperature forecast to reach 40 degrees in only two days' time, the streets and sidewalks will convert from mounds of snow to rivers of slush.

I am sitting in Sacred Heart Church. I usually do so at this time of the day during the work week. Noon Mass will begin in about five minutes. Sacred Heart Church has recently been designated a mission church in the diocese of Gary, meaning that it has no full-time pastor assigned. Rather, the pastor of nearby St. Mary of the Immaculate Conception administers the operation of the parish, but does so from St. Mary's. The number of families attending Sacred Heart finally dwindled to so few that it was deemed prudent to utilize its pastor at a parish where a greater number of families worshipped. However, not long ago, daily noon Mass, once celebrated at St. Mary's, was transferred to Sacred Heart. St. Mary's location, next to Marquette High School, made finding a parking place for noon Mass difficult. In order to alleviate the parking crunch, the noon Mass was pushed eight blocks to the north and west to Sacred Heart.

I have prayed Sext and prayed the Joyful Mysteries of the rosary. The usual cast of characters have arrived and have taken their accustomed seats. Old and young, infirm and robust, Opus Dei and Call to Action types all tumble together for this only show in town at noon. Beads rustle against pews, old ladies "whisper" prayers, babies coo and cry, home-school students plop down, businessmen slip in and scurry out, and it will all be over twenty minutes after the noon Angelus bell chimes.

How long ago New Melleray seems. For weeks after arriving home from retreat at New Melleray, the glow and excitement linger. How sweet was choir! How deep the prayer! But as the weeks stretch into months, excitement becomes memory, and memory eventually turns into simple recall. The next retreat available is many months away, and gumption for it cannot be generated. It's cold outside, the snow is piled up and the woman sitting behind me is sucking air through her false teeth so loudly that it makes my skin crawl.

So be it. New Melleray is my monastic home, but the world is my monastery. The streets I travel every day to and from work, and back and forth from church, *those* are my cloisters. My place in the pews at daily noon Mass and my seat at St. Joseph Church on Sundays, *that* is my choir. New Melleray is great, but here is where I belong.

For the new monasticism breeches the walls. The future cloister is beyond the enclosure. *Not* that the monastery as we now know it will fail, but what defines monastery will expand. The current explosion of oblate and associate groups, the ongoing proliferation of meditation and prayer groups mark just the beginning of this expansion. In the introduction to his book, *The Climate of Monastic Prayer*, Merton defines the monk as "a Christian who has responded to a special call from God, and has withdrawn from the more active concerns of a worldly life, in order to devote himself completely to repentance, 'conversion,' *metanoia*, renunciation, and prayer."[1] There is nothing in that definition that excludes the woman or man who lives in the city, suburbs or farm with spouse and children from being a monk. Of course, there is a difference between the canonical monk and the lay monastic, but that difference is one of degree. The degree of difference *does not* concern the fervor or devotion for God, but rather the degree to which the monastic tools are used to seek God.

The unifying point of this movement is that it is of the laity. Just as laymen and laywomen of the third and fourth centuries fled to the desert for a deeper experience of God, so now laywomen and laymen are coming together in cities and towns in order to taste the sweetness of the hidden God. Pockets of laity within parishes are probing the mystery with meditation, *lectio*, Office and patristics. As the clergy continue to dwindle in numbers, the laity's role in the church will increase. Lay monasticism is one part of that increase.

Danger, though, lurks afield. How do lay monastics insure themselves against veering off on their own private tangents? To whom or what is their monasticism accountable? How does the lay monastic guard against solipsism, or self-absorption? The danger is that the lay monastic will become filled with conceit, grow complacent and ignore the will of God in his or her life. How can the lay monastic in any way turn to God when she or he trusts only his or her own ideas on how to seek the Lord? God is not needed; only oneself is needed!

In the monastic houses a quite rigid, specific and orderly system of training and evaluation is in place to guide the progression of the person from postulant to solemnly professed. Though aspirants to the monastic orders may be few, the houses still take seriously Benedict's admonition that "admission to the religious life should not be made easy for newcomers."[2] Not so for the lay monastic; she or he must simply wing it. However, prudence dictates that lay monastics give formal direction to their lifestyle.

First, lay monastics must realize that this charism they enjoy does not emanate from themselves. It is a gift from God; therefore, the lay monastic is ultimately responsible to God. This may appear to be self-evident, but because lay monasticism in its present form is so highly individualistic, the tendency to believe that "I created and am in control of this lifestyle" is all too real and easy. Discernment is of utmost importance with the lay monastic, and the Scriptures are the voice of discernment. We must study the Scriptures. As the anonymous author of The Cloud of Unknowing wrote: "reading or hearing the word of God must precede pondering it and without time given to serious reflection there will be no genuine prayer."[3]

Second, prayer is the foundation of the life. "The whole purpose of the monk and indeed the perfection of his heart amount to this—total and uninterrupted dedication to prayer."[4] That about says it all. Yet, what form of prayer are we talking about? Benedict writes that "nothing comes before the Divine Office."[5] Therefore, the Liturgy of the Hours (Divine Office) is the prayer of precedence. Circumstance and occupation will dictate what Hours of the Office are consistently prayed. Some may be able to pray only Lauds, Vespers and Compline. Others may be so fortunate as to be able to pray all seven of the Hours. Whatever the number of hours prayed, perseverance in praying the Hours is essential.

Although praying the Hours takes precedence, it does not exhaust prayer. Two other forms of prayer should act as bookends for the central prayer of the Hours: *lectio divina* and meditation. From these forms of prayer all other types of prayer will flow. Armed with these forms of prayer the lay monastic is well on the way in fulfilling Saint Paul's dictum to "pray at every opportunity" (Ephesians 6:18).

The third way in which to hone the true monastic life is with spiritual direction from a competent spiritual director. The spiritual director may or may not be a monk. What is important is that the spiritual director be proven in the field of spiritual direction and be sympathetic to the charism of the lay monastic.

Fourth, the lay monastic must seek out brother and sister monastics. The final sentence in chapter four of *The Rule of St. Benedict* reads as follows: "But the workshop in which we diligently perform all these things [instruments of good works] is the seclusion of the monastery and our stability in the community."[6] We have seen that for the lay monastic the "monastery" can be anywhere. It is portable. The monastery can be the home, a room, an office. However, improvisation on community is not as easy. For the lay monastic "the community" is the problem—*there is little or no community*. Chances are good that lay monastics do not even know the whereabouts of other lay monastics. Even if the whereabouts of other lay monastics is known, distance between them may prevent their coming together on a regular basis. Another culprit working against meeting regularly is time. Lay monastics are, after all, laity. They live in the world of spouses, jobs and children, and all that goes with such obligations. Yet, it is vital that lay monastics do come together regularly. Monastics do not live in isolation from either the church at large or from other monastics. We are not lay *hermits*. The best avenue for discovering like-minded souls is becoming an oblate or associate of a monastic house. The Benedictines have for centuries welcomed oblates, and more recently the Cistercians have developed associate groups. These groups offer much needed support for those out there who are groping seemingly blindly for other monastics.

Finally, lay monastics should make use of *The Rule of St. Benedict*. It is a concise and practical book that has guided monastics for fourteen hundred years. Its commonsense approach is its strength. That it can be adapted to *lay monastics* is evident by the fact that Benedictines require its study by prospective oblates for a full year before making oblation.

Of course, the above suggestions do not exhaust all that can be done to help the lay monastic from straying from the true monastic path. Evagrius Ponticus, Saint John Cassian, the Desert Fathers, William of Saint-Thierry, *The Cloud of Unknowing* and a host of others should be read and digested.

The goal, however, is not the reading, nor the Hours, nor the meditation, nor some mythical romantic monastic ideal. God is the goal. Though we are powerless to grasp God, we nonetheless can know God—through love. Our spiritual ways are nothing if exercised without love. The spiritual exercises are not carried out in order to love God, but love of God impels carrying out the spiritual exercises. As Joan Chittister writes, "Monastic spirituality is a spirituality of love. It is a way of life, not a series of ascetical exercises."[7] Love God, love your neighbor and love in the manner in which Jesus loves you—unconditionally. Then will your sacrifice of praise rise up before the Lord like incense, like an evening oblation.

Sacred Heart Church is now about as full as it is going to get. Everyone is sitting in his or her usual spot. Sister Anna Clare and Sister Cyril are in front of me. Tom and his wife Sheryll and their baby daughter (with red hair) are seated on the other side of the aisle. Jeanne is behind me and to my right. Audrey and her brother sit one pew behind me and to my left. Soon, Jerome, the man who usually serves the noon Mass and proclaims the readings, will appear from the sacristy, followed by Father Till and Father McGrogan. What an eclectic bunch, this noon Mass crowd. A crowd that reflects the feast day which we celebrate this day, the Presentation. For just as Jesus was presented to the Lord in the temple to fulfill the law of Moses, so this crowd, this ragtag group of souls huddled in Sacred Heart Church in Michigan City, Indiana, on this cold February day is presented to the Lord by Jesus in order to fulfill the commandment of love—"do this in memory of me."

I am exploring more deeply, now. My soul approaches that region where dwells the silent semblance of God. My own identity is fading into the likeness of a strange and marvelous light; the solid world around me falling from view. Other forms draw near. The deeper I drift to the center of my soul, the farther I soar beyond myself, beyond my wants, beyond the clouds of heaven to encounter the Lord of Hosts at that center where heaven and earth embrace, where sinner and saint kiss. At the monastic center.

Bong! Bong! Bong! The noon Angelus rings out, and it all begins anew. "The angel of the Lord declared unto Mary, and she conceived of the Holy Spirit . . ."

*The Lord is my rock and my salvation. I shall cling
to him forever. For he protects me from my own
foolhardiness and loves me for no other reason than
I am his child. God is patient. God is mercy. And
when I stray I hear his voice calling my name, not
in anger, but in concern. Though he may seem to be
far away, he is at my elbow. I have only to turn,
and I shall see. His love is everlasting.*

NOTES

1 Thomas Merton, *Climate of Monastic Prayer* (Kalamazoo, Mich.: Cistercian Publications, 1969), p. 29.

2 *Rule of St. Benedict*, trans. Anthony C. Meisel and M. L. del Mastro (New York: Image, 1975), p. 93.

3 *The Cloud of Unknowing*, p. 9.

4 Saint John Cassian, *Conferences*, p. 101.

5 *Rule of St. Benedict*, p. 83.

6 *Ibid*, p. 54.

7 Joan Chittister, *The Rule of St. Benedict: Insights for the Ages* (New York: Crossroad, 1992), p. 56.

Appendix 1

Daily Schedule at New Melleray Abbey

Monday—Saturday

3:15 A.M.	Rise
3:30 A.M.	Vigils
4:00—6:30 A.M.	Private prayer, *lectio*, meditation
6:30 A.M.	Lauds
7:00 A.M.	Mass
7:45 A.M.	Breakfast
9:15 A.M.	Terce
9:30—11:15 A.M.	Morning work
11:45 A.M.	Sext
Noon	Dinner
1:45 P.M.	None
2:00—4:00 P.M.	Afternoon work
5:30 P.M.	Vespers
6:00 P.M.	Supper
7:30 P.M.	Compline
8:00 P.M.	Retire

Sunday

Same as above, except Mass is at 10:30 A.M., no Terce in the church and no work except for necessary chores.

Appendix 2

Psalm Schedule at New Melleray Abbey

Psalm Schedule Odd Weeks

	Sun	Mon	Tue	Wed	Thu	Fri	Sat
Vigils (3:30 A.M.)	17A 17B 17C 24 26 27	13 34 53 14 105A 105B	43A 43B 61 76 138A 138B	77A 77B 77C 11 41 + 42 83	57 58 59 136 143 144	3 7 15 88A 88B 88C	1 71 79 84 86 102
Lauds (6:30 A.M.)	50 117 150	49 5 110	72 42 111	101 63 114	100 87 113A	6 75 113B	37 142 112
Terce (9:15 A.M.)	118, I-IV	119, 120, 121					
Sext (11:45 A.M.)	118, V-VII	122 123 124	128 129 130	122 123 124	128 129 130	122 123 124	128 129 130
None (1:45 P.M.)	118, VII-XI	125 126 127	131 132	125 126 127	131 132	125 126 127	131 132
Vespers (5:30 P.M.)	109 2 46	18 47 95	67A 67B 96	45 135 97	9A 9B 98	21A 21B 92	44 137 23
Compline (7:30 P.M.)	4 and 90						

Psalm Schedule Even Weeks

	Sun	Mon	Tue	Wed	Thu	Fri	Sat
Vigils (3:30 A.M.)	28 29 30 33 65A 65B	36A 36B 51 10 104A 104B	106 55 69 70 74 81 93	A 106 B 60 73A 73B 80	12 25 48 78 82 141 143	16 54 108 A 108 B 139	8 18 44 45 47 71
Lauds (6:30 A.M.)	50 117 150	102 35 115	38 56 145	85 64 146	31 89 147	62 91 148	39 142 149
Terce (9:15 A.M.)	118, XII-XV	119, 120, 121					
Sext (11:45 A.M.)	118, XVI-XVIII	122 123 124	128 129 130	122 123 124	128 123 130	122 123 124	128 129 130
None (1:45 P.M.)	118, XIX-XXII	125 126 127	131 132	125 126 127	131 132	125 126 127	131 132
Vespers (5:30 P.M.)	109 2 46	19 20 95	103A 103B 96	134 140 97	32 40 98	68A 68B 99	23 84 22
Compline (7:30 P.M.)	4 and 90						

Appendix 3

Monasteries without Walls

Presentation to Convention 2000 of the American Benedictine Academy

St. Meinrad Archabbey
August 11, 2000
Sr. Antoinette Purcell, O.S.B., chair

I have been married twenty-four years to a woman I met when I was seventeen. She was sixteen when we met. We married one week shy of my twenty-third birthday. One week before the wedding my mother asked me if I were sure Sara was the one. I said yes. She asked how I knew. I replied, "I just know."

When Sara and I began dating back when we were students at New Albany High School, neither she nor I saw marriage to one another as the ultimate outcome of our dates to basketball games and movies and miniature golf courses. The relationship grew over time. Nearly a quarter of a century into our marriage, the relationship continues to grow. It will continue to grow until the day we die.

My interest, love and participation in monasticism did not spring forth suddenly. I did not rise one morning and say to myself, "You know, today I'm going to look into that monastic thing." As with the circumstances surrounding my first date with Sara, though, I can tell you the circumstances that drew my attention to monasticism. Browsing through the stacks in the library at Indiana University, one hot August afternoon, I came across a blue-covered volume. I flipped though the book and discovered these black and white pictures of monks and monasteries. On the inside cover of the book was the daily schedule these monks kept. This schedule said they rose at two o'clock in the morning and attended these church services with funny names—Terce, Sext, None (which I pronounced "none"). Now, I was intrigued. I mean, who *were* these guys and why would they do those things? I checked out the book and devoured it. The book was *The Waters of Siloe* by Thomas Merton.

Merton led to weekend retreats at Gethsemani, which pointed me to the Desert Fathers, which led to week-long retreats at Gethsemani, which led to my purchase of the Liturgy of the Hours, which led to *lectio* which introduced me to the twelfth-century Cistercians, which led to Centering Prayer, which spurred me to deeper and longer retreats at New Melleray, which led to meeting people in Northwest Indiana with like-minded interests. You see, it is all a process—gradual, mysterious, exciting, frustrating and wondrous, delving ever deeper, just as my relationship with Sara was and is.

But there is danger. Just as marriage can grow stale and become strained by selfishness, so monasticism—as practiced by those outside the monastery—can become filled with conceit, grow complacent and ignore the will of God by dissolving into merely self-love. How can the lay monastic in any way turn to God when he or she trusts only his or her own ideas on how to seek the Lord? In such cases, God is not needed—simply oneself! The monastic houses have in place a specific, orderly and firm system of training and evaluation to guide the progression of the person from postulancy to solemn vows. Benedict's admonition that "admission to the religious life should not be made easy for newcomers" is taken seriously. No such safeguards exist for the lay monastic. He or she alone is responsible for insuring against veering off on private tangents.

How to do that? First, lay monastics must realize that the charism they enjoy emanates from God, not from themselves. It is a gift from God; therefore, the lay monastic is ultimately responsible to God. This may appear self-evident, but because lay monasticism—in its present form—is so highly individualistic, the tendency is that it is all too real and easy to believe "I created and am in control of this lifestyle." Discernment, then, is of utmost importance, and the Scriptures are the voice of discernment.

Second, prayer is the foundation of the life. Saint John Cassian wrote that "the whole purpose of the monk and indeed the perfection of his heart amount to this—total and uninterrupted dedication to prayer." If the lay monastic is not praying, then he or she is not a monastic.

Third, take advantage of spiritual direction by a competent spiritual director.

Fourth, seek out fellow monastics. Hermits we are not. The final sentence in chapter four of *The Rule of St. Benedict* says, "But the workshop in which we diligently perform all these things [instruments of good works] is the seclusion of the monastery and our stability in the community." We will function better in a group. The best avenue that I know of for discovering like-minded souls is to become an oblate or associate of a house. I have made much progress in my spiritual life thanks to friendships with two men who are oblates of this monastery.

Finally, lay monastics should make use of *The Rule of St. Benedict*. That it can be adapted to *lay persons* is evident by the fact that Benedictines require its study by prospective oblates for a full year prior to making their oblation.

Monasticism beyond the walls is not readily recogniza-ble. This person dons no habit, wears no distinguishing ornament, lives not in a monastery. The parish pastor may issue an appeal for readers or Eucharistic ministers, but he is unlikely to issue an appeal for lay monastics. How, then, is this lifestyle, this movement to spread the gospel?

The answer is that it is already doing so. Though monasticism beyond the walls is not readily recognizable, it is very much alive. And it is growing. The May 26, 2000, issue of the *National Catholic Reporter* reports that there are 25,400 associates or oblates in America today. That figure is a 75 percent increase over figures tabulated in 1995. Furthermore, 84 percent of the 25,400 associates are women. The fact that this Convention feels the need to discuss the topic is evidence to the reality of monasticism beyond the walls.

Eugene Hensell, president of the ABA [American Benedictine Academy], writes in the current issue of the *American Monastic Newsletter* that "In more recent times our membership has begun to shift even further to include many more oblates and other people simply interested in the so-called 'monastic thing.' These members do not live in traditional monastic communities, yet they find monas-ticism, and especially monastic spirituality, very attractive."

People are hungry for God. As indifferent or even as antagonistic as our culture can be toward religion, people still yearn for the divine. For whatever reason, the institu-tional church—be it Roman Catholic, Orthodox or Protestant—is having trouble satisfying that yearning. Monasticism, though, seems to be filling the bill for a grow-ing number of people. And they are practicing monasticism in the station of life they are already in—which is primarily the lay state, many if not most, married and with children.

This may be confusing to some, but it is as right as rain

for monastics outside the walls. Jesus instructed us to love God and neighbor, and to love as he loves us—unconditionally. It just feels natural to monastics outside the walls to love God through loving spouse and children, and by celebrating that love not only by intimacy of husband and wife, but also by forms of prayer often associated with monks.

It seems to me that one of the great messages of monasticism outside the walls to the people of our time is that it breaks down the walls of compartmentalization. Our society is keen on putting religion in a cubbyhole, with visitation to that cubbyhole assigned only to a certain day, and then only to a few hours of that day. But the monk outside the walls shatters that mentality by showing that the demarcation between the holy and the secular is an illusion. The Incarnation has made all creation holy. Monastics outside the walls, in the very way they conduct their lives, are a living embodiment of that reality. *Not* that monasticism beyond the walls is the *sole* means to illustrate the holiness of all creation. Certainly, that reality can be lived in other ways. But monasticism beyond the walls is certainly *one* way to illustrate that the line between the secular and the holy is fiction. And as we've seen, it is a way that is growing rapidly.

It is too early to come to any sort of conclusion about the nature of the relationship between the monks on either side of the wall. In my conversations with some members of the community at New Melleray, I find some are wary of the associates and skeptical of what is called monasticism outside the walls; others there embrace it. All of this is too new. Time is needed to digest it and mull it over. I do suggest, though, that we are perhaps on the cusp of a new age in which the boundaries of the monastery will expand to such a point where reference to "wall" will be moot.

The goal is not the Liturgy of the Hours, nor the Desert Fathers, nor meditation or *lectio*, nor silence and solitude, nor Centering Prayer, nor some mystical romanticism of monasticism. The goal is love of God, union with God. William of Saint-Thierry wrote, "O the incalculable blessedness of the soul that merits so to be acted on by God, that through unity of spirit she loves in God, not just some property of his, but God himself, and even loves herself only in God!"[1] That is the goal of the monk. The tools of monasticism must never become ends in themselves. They are merely means to an end. By virtue of our baptism all are called to be holy. Many of us outside the walls believe that call to holiness in some strange way involves monasticism. How do we know that? We just know.

NOTE

[1] William of Saint-Thierry, *On Contemplating God, Prayer Meditations* (Kalamazoo, Mich.: Cistercian Publications, 1977), p. 48.